The Big Holy Book

The Big Holy Book

by Simon Mayo, Adrian Reith and Martin Wroe
Designed by Simon Gunn

Marshall Pickering
An Imprint of Harper Collins *publishers*

Marshall Pickering is an Imprint of
HarperCollins Religious
Part of HarperCollins Publishers
77-85 Fulham Palace Road, London W6 8JB

First published in Great Britain
in 1995 by Marshall Pickering

1 3 5 7 9 10 8 6 4 2

Copyright©1995, Simon Mayo, Adrian Reith and Martin Wroe

Simon Mayo, Adrian Reith and Martin Wroe assert the moral right
to be identified as the authors of this work

A catalogue record for this book is available from the British Library

0551 029218

Printed and bound in Great Britain by Scotprint Limited, Musselburgh, Edinburgh

CONDITIONS OF SALE

Can God cure your baldness? · Do vicars have souls? · Is there life before death? · Should men be ordained to the priesthood? · How do you become a saint? · Can you undo a fatwah? · Does God keep Sunday Special? · Is non-syncopated music of the devil? · Can you get divorced in church? · Does Desmond Tutu believe in ghosts? · Do young people believe in God? · Does She believe in them?

# Big Holy Hello

Welcome to The Big Holy Book, the most significant religious publication since The Satanic Verses. .

If you are a Radio One listener you may have heard of The Big Holy One, which began airing in the Spring of 1993 and merited a prestigious page three report in *The Sun* as the first religious series that Radio One had ever commissioned.

We called it 'irreligious religious radio' and guaranteed the minimum in talking dog-collars – with the exception of The Bishop and The Actress feature.

The programme, like this book, is interested in all kinds of strange beliefs, world views, religions and faiths. But it isn't Thora Hird or Harry Secombe territory and contains no known Songs of Praise.

Instead, The Big Holy One reports on people on the edges of faith, people tickling the underbelly of God who may not even know it at the time. From the Archbishop in a Tutu to East 17, from Waterboy, Mike Scott to material girl Madonna, the New Age to the middle aged, the Anglican Church to the Anglian Waterboard... rarely was religious broadcasting like this.

From the Top Five Religious Haircuts to chart-topping Ways to Die, from the invaluable Good Sects Guide to the critically acclaimed Heretic of the Week, pop stars were queuing up to receive their last judgement from Father Mayo.

No devout publication is complete without advertising and the royalties on this book are so derisory that we felt we had to turn to the great Church of the United States for help – its various members have paid for some beautiful, uplifting and inspirational advertising which decorates the following pages. Our thanks to The Wittenberg Door – and in particular its saintly editor Mike Yaconelli – for help in this delicate area.

Thanks also to His Holiness the Rt Rev Simon Parke – a future Archbishop of Tooting in the eyes of many observers – and to the Rt. Unrev Paul Powell of Spitting Image, and also the Archdeacon Malcolm Doney. Each has written many funny scripts for The Big Holy One, some of which we have included in the pages that follow. Thanks also to Hilary Bird who produced for radio much of the unholy writ that follows. And finally our holy design guru Simon Gunn without whom these pages would have been as boring as Leviticus.

So for the first time, in infallible and inspirational print, travel with us, Rev Holy Father Mayo and Holy Brothers Reith and Wroe, from the sublime to the religious in a matter of pages.

The Big Holy Book

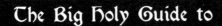

The Big Holy Guide to

Transcendental Meditation.

 **Maharishi Mahesh Yogi, an unknown Indian guru born in 1911, achieved overnight fame in 1967 when a pop group called the Beatles went to see him to study Transcendental Meditation.** Within a decade British followers had multiplied so rapidly that the movement bought Mentmore Towers, a stately home in Buckinghamshire, British capitol for the Maharishi's planned 'world government' which will "administer the age of enlightenment".

Followers are given a 'mantra', a secret chanting phrase which fits their personality and they aim to achieve transcendental consciousness. But that's just stage one of TM – next comes 'God consciousness' then 'union with God' and finally 'Brahma consciousness'

Followers of the Maharishi spent half a million pounds contesting 310 seats as The Natural Law Party in the 1992 General Election. They polled 64,000 votes.

The Maharishi – a Sanskrit title meaning 'great sage' – once named Glossop in Derbyshire as the mecca of TM. Followers claim to walk through walls, become invisible and fly but in 1985 one American sued the Yogi for $90,000 after injuring himself in the air.

GIVEN WHAT WE KNOW NOW

(A PUB)

DEREK: … And it's what the insurance guy called an 'Act of God'!

DAVE: … You don't believe in God, do you, Derek?

DEREK: Nah, Dave … can't believe in God these days – not given what we know now …

DAVE: Billions do though, mind …

DEREK: … Billions of flies eat dung, Dave …

DAVE: (LAUGHS)

DEREK: … I mean, a 'Supreme-All-Powerful-Being' maybe … given what we know now …

DAVE: Oh yeah, yeah, a 'Supreme-All-Powerful-Omnipresent-Being' … that's different innit … yeah …

DEREK: … a 'Supreme-All-Powerful-Being' who forced life out of the dead earth …

DAVE: … and pushed life into everything … yeah …

DEREK: … right … I'd go for a 'Supreme-All-Powerful-Being' who caused the world … everything in it … including us … and who is … here … in some way … I don't know how.

DAVE: (PAUSE) Like a sort of … 'God', you mean?

DEREK: God. Yeah. Like a sort of God. That's the right word. I mean, you have to go for that concept, don'tcha, given what we know now …

DAVE: Yeah. Right, right! Couldn't agree more … Derek

The Most Important Piece Of Furniture Your Family Will Ever Own

Christmas Tissue and Towels

☐ Guests are sure to get your holiday message when these adorn your bathroom. The white, standard-size toilet tissue roll is sprinkled with an all-over pattern of seasonal greetings in brilliant red. The three-ply towels are 12x17″, bright red with the design in white. They can also be used as festive dinner napkins, come in a pack of twelve.

H015-1-Toilet Tissue Roll $2.49
H016-1-Guest Towels, 1 pack, $1.39

Karl Wallinger of World Party

BHO: Browsing through your collected works … God, the devil, sin … they seem to be recurring themes. Presumably you're a regular church goer?

Heretic: Well I'm kind of non-denominational. I've kind of invented my own thing I guess.

BHO: Invented your own religion, what … *Wallingerism* ?

Heretic: I haven't invented my own religion, I've just invented my own particular journey that I'm travelling on.

BHO: Does that mean that you're absorbing bits and pieces from every religion?

Heretic: Not as we speak but on several occasions I've felt the need to ask big questions of myself and I haven't found that I've been particularly well-armed to answer them so I've looked to various places for that kind of guidance.

BHO: On the last album you sang, 'I'm into some God action and maybe yours is real, I need your God on my side.' Is that part of the quest?

Heretic: I don't mind a bit of God action of some sort y'know but I'm suspicious of organised religion.

BHO: What is it about organised religion?

Heretic: It's the funny clothes.

BHO: You're a rock'n'roll star, what are you talking about?

Heretic: You know what I mean. There was a man called Carl Jung, a Swiss psycho-analyst, and one of the interesting things he said which always rings a bell with me is 'I *know*, I don't need to

believe.' He was OK because he'd experienced what he called The State of Grace which meant that he sort of understood himself and had experienced the existence of God so he could believe in it.

BHO: Your religion or philosophy or whatever it is, could it be described as a kind of eco-religion, that's an ongoing theme in World Party songs.

Heretic: I think every religion has to be an eco-religion because I don't think anything would survive that proposed the disintegration of the environment – a 'trash the planet religion'.

BHO: Take 'Thank You World', one of the songs on your last album …

Heretic: Yeah, I have a spirit in me that seems to respond to a kind of natural-law type of thing, but it's tempered with a lot of other junk from man's history.

BHO: Bit of pantheism in there?

Heretic: Bit of pantheism, yeah, yeah … long panties …

BHO: Long panties as opposed to short ones?

Heretic: Yes, I do have a kind of pantheistic attitude, I am embroiled in that sort of natural vibe. There's a lot of people out there who would like something but have found themselves on the outside just because of the times we live in. A lot of the churches in England are like Victorian buildings with sort of strange old tunes going on in them which I actually like …

BHO: Being a purveyor of strange old tunes yourself, what is it you like? What

Big Holy Chart

Top Fundamentalist Short-Cuts to Making Sure You Behave Properly

You get publically whipped if you're caught sipping a shandy, you get your arm cut off if you're caught with your hand in the till, you get your willie cut off if you're caught with it in the woman next door's till, you get your eye pulled out if you're caught looking lustfully at a member of the opposite sex (both eyes if its a member of the same sex), you get your church membership cut off (ie. excommunicated – ouch!) – if you don't believe everything the Pope tells you and you get your life cut off (a Fatwah) if you blaspheme against the Prophet.

I WOULD NEVER BE WITHOUT THE IDEA THAT THERE WAS SOME HIDDEN FORCE THAT WAS RESPONSIBLE FOR CREATION. I WOULDN'T BE SATISFIED WITH BEING A HUMANIST AND THINK-ING THAT IT'S JUST ME AND MY BRAIN AND MY THOUGHTS.

Strange But True

The Exclusive Brethren, an offshoot of the Plymouth Brethren, objected to the European Community in Brussels that a widely used EC standards mark could represent the Antichrist. The Community is known as CE on the continent and the CE logo, says the sect, corresponds uncomfortably with predictions in the Book of Revelation – it believes that the Beast of Revelation is in fact Europe.

The EC were not convinced and remained resolutely unbelieving. They refused to promise the Exclusive Brethren exclusion from the rules and from the 'mark of the Beast'.

appeals to you?

Heretic: I'm quite a fan of the High Church in a way. There's something more ethereal and spiritual in it. If I was making an ad and wanted to give an atmosphere of spirituality I'd put disembodied choirboys voices somewhere in a huge chapel with some stained glass windows. I don't know whether I'd have a lot of people raving around with a twelve string and a Yamaha synth.

BHO: A bit like World Party!

Heretic: Not really, it doesn't really do it for me.

BHO: You distrust organised religion and yet there's obviously something there.

Heretic: There's definitely an element of power seeking – say within the history of the Catholic Church – which isn't totally above-board. But I could probably hand you over to my friend Sinead on that one. I'm suspicious of soul-grabbing, like the Mormon thing about typing everybody's details into the computer and saying, 'Yup, they're a Mormon now.' It just seems like a big numbers game. What's going on guys, I thought this was meant to be peace and love?

BHO: The single 'Is it Like Today' is very philosophical and again God turns up in one of the verses?

Heretic: I would never be without the idea that there was some higher power – not power but some other hidden force – that was responsible for creation. I wouldn't be satisfied with being a humanist and thinking that it's just me and my brain and my thoughts. That doesn't satisfy me as any kind of explanation. But I have enjoyed thinking about things with my feet firmly on the ground – that's the way

I see it with my impoverished thought-waves.

BHO: As you are our heretic of the week you have to choose your chosen method of torture before we finish, what would that be?

Heretic: I thought of something but then I thought I can't possibly say that.

BHO: Well try me.

Heretic: No, no I ...

BHO: Try me

Heretic: No, I'll do another one ...

BHO: Try me.

Heretic: No honest, honest, it was just too much. I would have deserved to have been burnt at the stake if I'd said that.

BHO: Go on.

Heretic: It was something to do with young ladies but I won't go into it.

BHO: It doesn't sound like a torture particularly.

Heretic: Well it would have been honestly, I tell you. To find that I'm woken up in the morning and I'm on a six-foot leash and my cigarettes are eight feet away from me would probably be the ultimate horror.

BHO: We'll see if we can arrange that.

LIFE IS RATHER LIKE A TIN OF SARDINES – WE'RE ALL OF US LOOKING FOR THE KEY. **ALAN BENNETT, PLAYWRIGHT**

JANE: I don't know what I'm going to do about this stain, Marge.

MARGE: Let's have a look, Jane. Mmm, nasty. What is it?

JANE: Adultery.

MARGE: Long term?

JANE: Yes. I've been abusing Trevor's trust for several months now, but the guilt's gone deep-down.

MARGE: Not for long, Jane. (ZING!)

JANE: But it's a fracture in my soul, Marge.

MARGE: And this, Jane, is new Coverup. Watch.

JANE: But the stain's still there, Marge.

MARGE: Stain? What stain? I can only see Coverup. (LAUGHING)

JANE: (laughing) Oh Marge, where would I be without your nihilistic secular philosophy! I feel worse already! (kitchen laughter)

MVO: Stains, what stains? – with new, fast-acting Coverup. You know it doesn't make sense.

Sounds of Blackness

The Last Judgement

BHO: **Do you have to have faith to sing Gospel?**

Blackness: **Absolutely, the Gospel is the good news and the good news without faith … it's impossible to please God. The two go together.**

BHO: **Do you have to have faith to enjoy gospel?**

Blackness: **I don't think so, we've been told by people of different faiths or of no faith that the music is a positive force in their lives, that they can appreciate it aesthetically, that it's motivated or uplifted them.**

BHO: **Do you have to be black to sing Gospel?**

Blackness: **You don't have to be but it helps. There are many non-black Gospel singers but in terms of authenticity it certainly is an African-American style of music.**

BHO: **What music would you like at your funeral?**

Blackness: **Some foot-stomping, hand-clapping, feel-that-music songs …**

BHO: **Are you going to Heaven?**

Blackness: **Absolutely, it's in his book … I know because I've accepted Jesus Christ as my personal Saviour and I'm on my way.**

BHO: **If Guns and Roses invited you to sing with them, would you?**

Blackness: **No …**

BHO: **Who are your favourite preachers?**

Blackness: **The Reverend Jesse Jackson.**

BHO: **Have you ever fallen asleep in Church? …**

Blackness: **Oh, I may have had an occasional nod over the years.**

"Wouldn't it be so much easier for people like me if God just came in, sat down here with us and offered me a cigarette. Then everyone would know."

Caroline Quentin of The National Theatre and divers sit-coms in conversation over tea and cucumber sandwiches with the Right Rev Roy Williamson, the Bishop of Southwark.

Actress: Here's a sticky one then, the ultimate question: does God exist? Can you prove to me that He, or indeed She, exists?

Bishop: Well I hope God exists because if He doesn't, I'm out of a job. But yes, I know that God exists: as far as its possible for me to know anything: because I think there's evidence around that he does.

Actress: Really?

Bishop: Well for instance there's the whole question of order in the world though I have to admit there's some chaos as well.

Actress: You've seen my wardrobe!

Bishop: And there's the question of design and the whole question of the moral nature of people, the feeling that they ought to be doing things. These things seem to me to point to the fact that behind the universe there is a God.

Actress: Wouldn't it be fantastic, and so much easier for people like me who don't really know, if God just came in, sat down here with us and offered me a cigarette or poured me a cup of coffee. Then everyone would know and I could say, 'It's alright I've seen him it's fine, relax, join in.'

Bishop: Well you can't prove God by putting him in a test tube and testing him like that. He's not a mathematical problem, you can't prove him beyond a shadow of doubt like that ... but as to a question of whether God could come and actually reveal himself in terms that people could understand unmistakeably, there is a sense in which he has done that

and he did that at Bethlehem: that was the whole point of Christmas; that God took flesh, God took a personality …

Actress: I know, but that was so long ago, I mean I wasn't there.

Bishop: But I'm here with you today and I'm one of his mates!

Actress: Yeah but you're not the baby Jesus are you?

Bishop: No of course not, but nevertheless my life has been transformed by Jesus. I'm here today because I'm following Jesus and part of his instructions to me are to share his love and to share his faith so in another sense he has no hands but my hands, no voice but my voice, no heart but my heart.

Actress: Do you know what I'd like, my darling? I'd like it if God did a great big miracle that I could witness. Why don't we ever see great big miracles now like the parting of the Red Sea or water into wine and all that sort of stuff? I'd love that. It's so dramatic.

Bishop: Yes. He did something very dramatic you know when Jesus rose from the dead. That was the greatest miracle and the greatest sign that there ever was

Actress: Better than Paul Daniels.

Bishop: And that's why I'm a Christian you see, because that actually happened and I encountered or was encountered by a Jesus who is alive … when I speak about Jesus I'm not talking about somebody who lived 2,000 years ago, but actually somebody who's alive today and who encounters me day after day, so for me the miracle has happened. Of course there are other miracles and there are people who will tell you that they have experi-

enced miracles of healing and reconciliation in their own lives. It's a difficult question. I think it was Prince who said, 'God's a funky little dude because everybody's looking for him and no-one can find him.'

Actress: A bit like my husband. But look at this newspaper. In Bosnia a thousand dead; atrocities in Northern Ireland; bombs in India, and the root cause of it all: religion. Why should anybody bother with religion when it clearly just divides people?

Bishop: I think we've got to get it straight, there are religious people everywhere, there's bound to be religious people on both sides of any particular divide, but the question is this: is it religion that starts it? Now I think of my situation in Northern Ireland where for twenty years we've been living with this kind of thing but people think that it is a holy war between Catholics and Protestants.

Actress: And is it not?

Bishop: No, it's not. No, it's not. Ninety five per cent of the people are not involved in any kind of violence and there's Roman Catholics and Protestants among them. I happen to be for instance, a child of a mixed marriage, my father was a Protestant my mother Roman Catholic. It's not a religious or holy war it's simply ideology, it's a cultural divide and there's evil men and women on both sides of the divide who are simply using religion, and the excuse of religion to cause trouble.

Actress: But Christians have waged wars haven't they?

Bishop: Oh they have, and people are forever, and quite rightly so, pointing to the Inquisition and so on, but you know

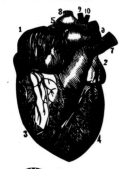

GOOD OLD C OF E

JRF: Excuse me, Vicar, I'm looking for a book called *Heart Surgery* by JR Flyfisherman …

VICAR: Sorry. But we've got a nice one about flower arranging … and jumble sales …

JRF: Oh, God! I'm having a heart attack!

VICAR: We do have *The Very Best of Brassrubbing* in hardback …

Announcer: Good Old Church of England. Not just there for the little things in life like a burial or a positive AIDS test. We're also a pretty place to get married.

Marxism and Capitalism and greed, and all that springs of it, has caused more violence and more deaths in the world than religion ever has.

Actress: Both sides, and not just in relation to Northern Ireland, but both sides say that God is on their side, that they're fighting for God. That must worry you?

Bishop: Well it does actually and in a sense that's my trouble. I say to myself, 'If I wasn't a bishop, would I come here?' and the answer I get back isn't very complimentary.

Actress: So are people still going to church? How are your seats, how are your bookings? What's your box office like?

Bishop: Box office? Quite good. Don't

Bishop: It's a difficult question. I think it was Prince who said, 'God's a funky little dude because everybody's looking for him and no-one can find him.'

there's no easy answer to it. It happens, it happens within the church you see. You think of a thing like the debate about the ordination of women. There are those who are for it saying God's on our side, and those against it are saying God's on our side and he can't be on both sides at once. Once we tie God down to be in our particular box, doing our particular thing, at our particular time, he ceases to be God.

Actress: I know this is an absurd question with you sitting there in your dog-collar, but would you describe yourself as a religious person?

Bishop: No, I'm not.

Actress: No!

Bishop: No, I'm not. The hardest question for a bishop to answer or for me to answer honestly, is do I like going to church, so don't ask me that either.

Actress: Do you like going to church?

Bishop: I have to go to church too often,

believe all this talk about the church being in serious and terminal decline. I don't believe one word of it. Every time I go to church I find crowds there. It might be because I'm there but I don't think so.

Actress: You don't have to fight to get a

Actress: A bit like my husband.

ticket though I don't believe. Tell me, is God a loving God?

Bishop: Yes, that's my belief and conviction and experience.

Actress: Is he all powerful?

Bishop: There is a sense in which yes, he is all powerful but that doesn't mean he can do absolutely everything. He can't contradict himself ...

Actress: He can't tap dance ...

Bishop: ... he may not be able to but he can help other people to tap dance. His rhythm's quite good you know, the seasons: he gets them in the right order.

Actress: If he's so loving and almost all powerful, why does he allow so many people to suffer?

Bishop: Well you know that is the crunch question …

Actress: I know. It's a ghastly question to ask you, isn't it my darling.

Bishop: It's the proper question to ask a bishop but bishops have got to be honest and therefore I'll be honest with you. I could not answer that in a totally satisfactory way and no-one since the beginning of time has been able to answer that in a totally satisfactory way. But in one sense Caroline, I think the question may need to be re-phrased a bit because, I don't think that God allows suffering in the sense that he's got his little book and he says, 'Well, she'll have flu today and

> *"Do you know what I'd like my darling? I'd like it if God did a great big miracle that I could witness. Why don't we ever see great big miracles now like the parting of the Red Sea or water into wine and all that sort of stuff?"*

he'll have something else tomorrow.' If God created a materialistic universe which means that it's a universe where things can go wrong, and if God gave people free will, then suffering is almost inevitable.

Actress: Do we cause our own suffering?

Bishop: No, we don't. Some people do by the way they live, by the things they do, but there are lots of people, innocent people, children, who don't and that's where the problem comes in.

Actress: Do you ever question? Do you sometimes think, 'This just isn't fair, this darling person is ill.' Do you ever question that?

Bishop: Yeah. Two things here: I was in Bradford at the time of the great fire disaster, and was heavily involved in the aftermath of that. Now that was a terrible occasion and certainly at that particular time it shook faith to the foundations. Just a year later I had a massive heart attack.

Actress: You did?

Bishop: Yeah, I was here in London at the General Synod so perhaps there was an excuse for it, but I had a heart attack and was rushed into Westminster Hospital and was very close to death, and as I began to come out of that I began to ask God, 'Well, what on earth are you playing at?' Yet I came through that with my faith stronger and with my love for life all the greater … that's the thing.

Actress: So when you asked him that question, 'Why have you done this to me?' what answer did he give you?

Bishop: None for a while.

Actress: Really, it went very quiet? He probably thought you needed the rest …

Bishop: I suddenly began to realise that there were people who valued me as a person, valued my work, and were concerned about me. Sometimes you only read about that from heaven in your obituary …

Actress: And you had it all straight in front of you.

Bishop: It was anticipated yeah.

Actress: Talking of suffering and people who suffer, how's your congregation?

Bishop: Suffering … (laughs) …

Actress: On my way to the theatre I pass mosques, synagogues and churches and it struck me that all these religions lead to the same God. Well, they may give him different names, God, Allah, Jahweh, or whatever … but aren't they all worshipping the same God?

Bishop: Certainly if we're talking about the three that you mentioned, Moslems, Jews and Christians, there is a sense in which the religions do spring from the same source and the Scriptures and the God of the Scriptures is the person whom they recognise.

Actress: Does it make any difference to you whether nor not someone is a Christian. Do you think everyone should be a Christian? Does it not make any difference because they're all headed in the same direction really?

Bishop: If I said that to a Jew or a Moslem he'd be very annoyed because it seems to me that the only way you can talk about your God with integrity is to believe in him and to believe in him 100%. I would not want to be arrogant before my Moslem and Jewish friends and say Christianity is better than yours …

Actress: My God is better than your God, yah booh sucks.

Bishop: My Daddy can beat your Daddy. I would want to say that this is my strong conviction, I believe that the God whom I follow is the true God.

Actress: I have to ask you then, what's going to happen to people like me, people who are non-Christian, who have no religion when they pop their clogs … will they go upstairs…?

Bishop: I must put it like this; I believe it with all my heart though not everybody agrees with me: there are many people outside the Church who nevertheless are followers of God in that they are not quite sure, but they are prepared to follow whatever light they have got. I've discovered out in society many people who never come to Church, wouldn't call themselves a Christian, a Jew or a Moslem, but whose lives actually reveal the character of Christ.

But as regards to those who have actually opposed God or opposed Christianity, I don't know the answer to that, I simply leave them to the mercy of God.

Actress: You don't think that if you are a Moslem you will burn in Hell …

Bishop: I will be very surprised if anyone burns in hell …

Actress: If you don't think that anyone goes to hell, does that mean that everyone will go to heaven …

Bishop: I didn't say that people didn't go to hell, I'm anxious about this idea of burning in hell. I can't actually believe in a God who is going to punish people eternally, if by hell is actually meant that God, at the end of it all, will respect the choices people have made. And remember God is a person who respects people: and if people make a genuine sincere choice to dispense with the services of God, God may respect that and say, 'okay …'

> **"Marxism and Capitalism and Greed have caused more violence and deaths than religion ever has."**

ON TRANS-CONTINENTAL FLIGHTS I WOULD RECITE THE LORDS PRAYER TO MYSELF ON TAKE-OFF AND LANDINGS. ONE DAY I FOUND MYSELF MURMURING, "OUR FATHER, WHICH ART IN HEAVEN, HOLLY-WOOD BY THY NAME," AND RE-ALISED IT WAS TIME TO GET OUT.

Steven Bach, Film Producer.

WHITE IS THE VIRGINAL COLOUR, SYMBOLISING PURITY AND INNOCENCE. WHY DO NUNS WEAR BLACK?
DAVE ALLEN

The Big Holy Guide to
The Church of Scientology

The Church of Scientology, founded by a science fiction writer who claimed that he was killed twice during the war, boasts 700 centres in 65 countries and 8 million members including Tom Cruise, Nicole Kidman, John Travolta and Lisa Marie Presley.

The Church teaches that people are basically good but have been messed up by past experiences and that only Scientology can cure them. It also says a mother must be silent in child-birth to avoid damaging the mind of the baby.

Salvation comes by visiting an Auditor who will examine you with his E-Machine, a kind of lie-detector for stress, invented by L Ron Hubbard – the science fiction writer.

It can cost up to £300 to visit an auditor.

'Scientology contains the secrets of the universe.' said John Travolta. 'That may be hard for people to handle, hearing that.'

Big Holy Chart

Top Five Religious Fashion Items

At five it's the sober suit and shiny black shoes of the Baptist minister, dressing the way the Apostle Paul did. Down three at four it's the ever popular Jesus Sandals – for that sincere and concerned summer look. Straight in at three it's the Mitre, the hat to balance on your head if you're a Bishop who really wants to Get Episcopal. Still at two it's the veil: no well-dressed Moslem sister can be seen without one in more and more countries.

And new at number one in this week's top religious fashion items is the Black Cassock, the long dress-like garment that hundreds of clergy slip into Sunday by Sunday. Some do it mid-week too – don't be shy.

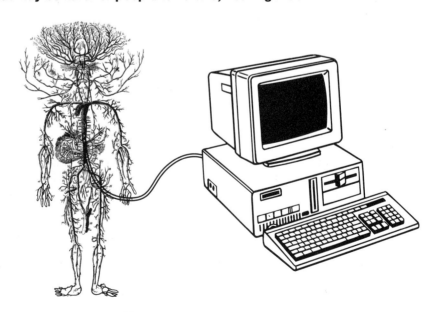

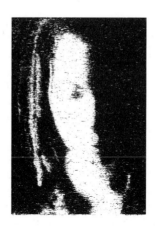

 # Terence Trent D'Arby

The Last Judgement

BHO: **What music would you like played at your funeral?**

TTD: **I would like the oboe concerto from Mozart. Actually a lot of it would be classical music and then afterwards I would hope that a lot of great pop music and rock music and jazz would be played and people could celebrate.**

BHO: **Have you ever had a religious experience?**

TTD: **I would say that I have had very spiritual and very mystical experiences, I wouldn't call them religious experiences.**

BHO: **Do you ever pray?**

TTD: **In my own way I would say yes, as I believe that the path to that force that drives the universe whatever we wish to call it, I believe the first doorway lies within ourselves.**

BHO: **Are you going to heaven?**

TTD: **I feel I'm already in heaven ... as Jesus said, 'the kingdom of heaven is all around you.'**

BHO: **Does being the son of a Bishop make you like Church, more, or less?**

TTD: **I think it made me aware of how spiritual I am as a person, even though I can honestly say – and not just because he's my father – that I never saw my father practice anything different from what he preached, I saw a lot of stuff that perhaps put me off.**

BHO: **Does God have a colour?**

TTD: **Yes. He is the colour of your heart.**

BHO: **Who's the holiest person you've ever met?**

TTD: **Potentially anybody I meet. You; myself ... I don't want to be ... that's not a facetious answer.**

BHO: **Does the devil have all the good tunes?**

TTD: **No, but he has all the good rhythms.**

Does God have a colour?

Yes. He is the colour of your heart.

I AM A HOLY LOAF. I WENT TO CHURCH SCHOOL AS WELL AS A CHRISTIAN COLLEGE BUT I HAD REAL PROBLEMS

Meatloaf

BHO: Can I call you the Holy Loaf?

Meatloaf: I think that if you feel like calling me that, that is absoloutely OK.

BHO: So Holy Loaf, thank you for coming in to the Big Holy One. I saw you on the television last week and you said that you reckon you're the reincarnation of Henry VIII. Is this true?

Holy Loaf: Oh ... you know that I was once told this by a psychic and then I was told this by another psychic and I've been told this by three psychics and I don't even ask them the question. I'm not even there to see the psychic! I don't deal with that kind of stuff.

BHO: So do you take it seriously?

Holy Loaf: Well I've taken it seriously enough that my wife and I went to see where Henry VIII was buried, we've been to Hampton Court, we've got all these Henry VIII books, we've got a Henry VIII statue ...

BHO: So you do take it seriously then?

Holy Loaf: Well sort of, not really. I don't know whether to take reincarnation seriously or not. I have a big religious background here. My mother and her sisters were a gospel quartet, they used to sing the gospel at the end of a taped Bing Crosby radio show and they did a lot of touring as a gospel group. My grandfather was a minister, I studied the Bible in school. When the test came round I had like the eleventh highest grade in America on the Bible quizes. A little known fact there.

BHO: So you really are a big Holy Loaf?

Holy Loaf: I am a holy loaf! I went to Church School as well as a Christian College. I had real problems though, 'cause I grew up going to church – Sunday morning, Sunday night,

Wednesday night services they used to have. I don't go to church now but my wife and I teach the kids about the Bible and things like that because that's important. But the Church actually became very hypocritical to me. What the people would do in the church on Sunday and what they would do outside on a Friday night ... I didn't exactly like that part. So I said I don't think I want to be part of an organised religion. I don't think that God intends you to do that, I don't think that it's necessary to believe in God and believe in Jesus or whatever and be a part of some organised trip. If you want to get serious for a minute, which I think I can, everyone can serve God and Jesus in their own way without telling everyone that they're doing it, and I'm not saying that the people who do tell everyone that they're doing it are wrong. I'm saying that I get bummed sometimes by the guys on the streetcorners and I'll walk past and they'll say (preacher voice), 'You're going to hell', and I go, 'No I'm not.'

BHO: It's been nice to meet you Big Holy Loaf.

Holy Loaf: This is it? This is it? We're ending? I just got here! (strident preacher voice) See I wownted to tell you brother; what I wownted to do here todaaay, was to tell you 'bout brother Loaf! I wownted to tell you 'bout Jeeeysurs! I wanted to tell you about the Glooowry! I wanted to tell you about the Salvaayshun that is at hand! But since we do not, we do not we do not seeeym to have tiaaam for this thing today I will come back, I will be here, I will see you again brother!

BHO: Thank you Meat!

God is really only another artist. He invented the giraffe, the elephant and the cat. He has no real style. He just goes on trying other things.

Pablo Picasso, painter

Strange But True

A Buddhist priest solemnly chanted prayers to the 'souls' of thousands of used brassieres in a ceremony wishing the women's undergarments a peaceful afterlife in heaven.

The priest knelt before a pyramid of about 20,000 bras piled high at Tokyo's Zojoji Temple by bra manufacturer Triumph International (Japan) Limited. 'The memorial service is held to express our gratitude for the bra which is one of the most important items for women,' a Triumph spokesman said. 'And we wish this event will have women take a new look at bras that influence feminine attraction.'

To celebrate its 100th anniversary, Triumph collected 200,000 bras from Japanese women in a two-month campaign where the manufacturer gave women a pair of 'Sloggi' panties for every two bras turned in.

As the priest ended his prayers, dry ice billowed from under the pyramid and thousands of bubbles rose from behind as the Yokohama City University Mixed Chorus broke into a rendition of Mozart's Ave Verum Corpus. The company later incinerated the undergarments.

Big Holy Chart

Top Five Ways to Spot a Member of an Obscure Religious Cult

In at five this week it's the glazed look and coat-hanger-in-gob smile as they wander up to you in the street. At number four it's that invitation to contribute to 'medical research in the third world'. At three it's the shifty man with a biro and a clip-board 'conducting a survey into religious beliefs'. At two it's that old favourite, an invitation back for supper. (But will you ever be able to leave again?)

But at number one in this week's ways of spotting a member of an obscure religious cult it's anyone with a dog-collar, big black book or powerful pong of incense who says he's against the ordination of women. He is almost certainly against any position for women except the missionary one.

Can you spot the Big Holy Brother? Hold the book up to your nose and pray hard.

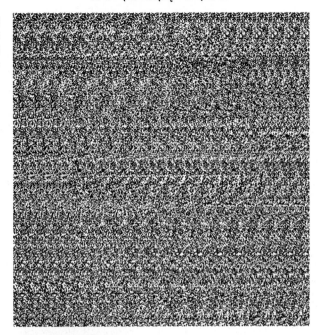

MEANING

TEACHER: ... And just what's the meaning of this?

PUPIL: Well, it's a noun, isn't it sir?

TEACHER: What is?

PUPIL: 'This' sir.

TEACHER: What the hell are you talking about, Meldrup?

PUPIL: You asked me what the meaning of 'this' was, sir.

TEACHER: I didn't mean THAT!

PUPIL: No, I know, sir, you meant 'THIS'.

TEACHER: I didn't mean 'this' either Meldrup!

PUPIL: Then what DID you mean, sir?

TEACHER: You know perfectly well what I was ... (fades out)

ANNOUNCER: The Church of England. Where the meaning of this, that and indeed the other becomes gloriously apparent.

Strange But True

Jesus of the Sandstorm

The American newspaper *Weekly World News* reports that the Face of Jesus has been seen over Somalia by a US Marine and that religious experts had called it a miracle. Correspondent Becky Granger reported that the face of Jesus appeared in a sandstorm over the African country as a message of hope to thousands of starving citizens as well as US Marines heading up Operation Restore Hope.

The 500 foot image was snapped by one soldier and the paper reports that Pope John Paul describes it as 'a sign from God'.

The photographer said, 'I'm not the most religious guy in the world but I know Jesus Christ when I see him.'

The newspaper made no comment on why the photograh of Jesus in the Sandstorm looked remarkably like that of actor Robert Powell who played Christ in Franco Zeffirelli's film Jesus of Nazareth.

Big Holy Chart

Top Five Fatuous Religious Observations

Holding on at number five is 'That Mother Teresa's a marvel'. Yes, true but she's not the only one you know. Up at four it's that old chestnut 'Religion's for those who need a crutch' – okay, but who isn't limping? Straight in, kind of loopily at three is 'It's amazing how accurate those star charts are sometimes'. Yes, about as amazing as a coin landing on 'Heads', fifty per cent of the time. Up, sleep-inducingly, at two is 'Everyone who goes to church, synagogue or mosque is a hypocrite.' Of course they are, but there's always room for one more. And finally, still there at number one, the most fatuous religious comment of the week is 'World religions are really all the same'. Which is undeniably true of course ... apart from the huge differences between them all.

Heretic Suzanne Vega

IF YOU'RE HAVING A PROBLEM WITH SOMEONE WHAT THEY WILL USUALLY TELL YOU IS TO CHANT FOR THEIR HAPPINESS. THE IDEA IS THAT THROUGH YOUR OWN INDIVIDUAL HAPPINESS YOU CONTRIBUTE TO WORLD PEACE.

Suzanne Vega

BHO: Suzanne, you've been brought up a Buddhist. Which particular sect in Buddhism is that?

Heretic: It's the Nichiren Shoshu sect of Buddhism.

BHO: So how does that differ from the main strand of Buddhism?

Heretic: It's not really as though there is a main strand of Buddhism. I think there are a lot of different sects and a lot of different practices. This one is different as it has an active practice in that you chant and do prayers twice a day as opposed to the more reclusive kinds of Buddhism where you medidate or you withdraw from society.

BHO: So what do you chant ... 'blood makes noise?'

Heretic: No, you don't chant, 'blood makes noise'. Definitely not – unless you want to get horrible anxiety. No, you chant, 'Nam yo re henge cho ...' That means I devote my life to the mystic law of simultaneous cause and effect through ·sound – if you want the very shallow translation.

BHO: Sounds pretty deep to me. And who are you chanting to ... yourself?

Heretic: When you become a Buddhist you receive a scroll and you have it enshrined in your house and you have an altar and you chant to the scroll which in its simple form represents your highest life within you. But you need to chant outside of yourself. It's not enough just to chant within yourself, you have to look at the object ... it's a little bit more complicated than I can go into here ... but you're chanting to the scroll on the wall in front of you.

BHO: What are you chanting for, for your own personal happiness or do you use it in more conventional prayer kind of style where you're actually chanting for something else?

Heretic: Usually you're doing both, in fact if you're having a problem with someone what they will usually tell you is to chant for their happiness. The idea is that through your own individual happiness you contribute to world peace. You are

encouraged to chant for anything you would like to, meaning that if you don't have food you are encouraged to chant for that, you are encouraged to chant for your rent money ... but at the same time also for those higher things like compassion or understanding.

BHO: And does it work?

Heretic: Yes.

BHO: Is it the same as positive thinking?

Heretic: I don't think so because there's a more active, physical aspect to it, you actually pray, and you read the Sutra. The prayer in the morning takes 25 minutes and in the evening takes 15 minutes.

BHO: Were you brought up a Buddhist?

Heretic: My family went to its first meeting when I was 16 years old and we have been practising more or less ever since then as a family.

BHO: Not a conventional American religious upbringing ...

Heretic: My family is a very unconventional family. My step-father's father was a minister and was brought up in a very strict religious family and he was very rebellious and what appealed to him about Buddhism is that you can chant for very practical things.

BHO: Do any particular moral values come with your sect of Buddhism, does it affect the way you behave and relate to other people, the way you perform your songs?

Heretic: It makes you aware that most people want the same things in life, to be treated fairly, to have enough to eat, to have enough money, and to have a good relationship with husband or wives or partners ...

BHO: A lot of people would have those attitudes without having any faith at all ...

Heretic: I suppose you're right, most people could cultivate those attitudes on their own, but I found it did make a great difference in my life.

BHO: Are there any Buddhist jokes, because there are lots of Church of England jokes ...

Heretic: Oh my God ...

BHO: Which god is that, Buddha ...?

Heretic: No, I hadn't meant to say that ...

BHO: Can you say that ...

Heretic: You can say, 'Oh my God but it doesn't mean the same in the Buddhist belief system. it's not as if there is not a God but its not one that we worship.

BHO: Can you blaspheme against him ... or her?

Heretic: You can pretty much say what you want to and you can wear leather and you can eat meat ... they leave it all up to you to behave in the way that you want to ... so you can say, 'Oh my God, but it's not the most tactful thing to be saying.'

BHO: Any Buddhist jokes?

Heretic: Well, they'd be too 'in' for you to get ... Jokes about your karma coming out and this kind of thing ... I'm afraid that I'm not up on the latest Buddhist jokes ...

BHO: As you are the heretic of the week Suzanne, I do have to ask you if you'd like to give us your chosen method of torture ...

Heretic: It would be putting me in a room with all my books and not be able to read them for a week ...

BHO: We can arrange it, thank you for being our heretic ...

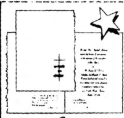

The Big Holy Guide to

The Mormons

 Members of The Church of the Latter Day Saints believe that Jesus visited America after his resurrection and that he will establish his Kingdom in the USA – in particular in Salt Lake City, Utah.

The Church of the Latter Day Saints was founded by Joseph Smith, born in Vermont in 1805, who claimed God appeared to him when he was 14.

Three years later the angel Moroni told Jo he would find a book written on gold plates telling the history of the early Americans and the complete gospel. Jo dictated The Book of Mormon before Moroni took back the plates.

When it was published the Church of Jesus Christ of the Latter Day Saints was founded, but Joseph – often mocked for his claims – died in a gunfight in prison in 1844.

Donny and Marie Osmond – and their famous brothers – are the worlds most famous Mormon missionaries and, like other Mormons, believe that only Mormons will get to the third and highest heaven.

True Mormons give a tenth of their income to the Church, fast once a month and don't smoke or drink. Some fringe Mormons have several wives too. Joseph's Smith's successor Brigham Young had 17.

If are not a Mormon yet do not despair – you can be baptised by proxy after you are dead.

E17

The Last Judgement

BHO: Good evening to you Tony and here are your questions. Question one. Have you ever had a religious experience?

E17 Tony: Mmm no. I don't really know what a religious experience is. I guess I'd define it as a spiritual experience and we have spiritual experiences every day, so yeah, I'm sure I have.

BHO: Is it true you have an altar in your bedroom?

E17 Tony: Mmm. No! I have a bed in my bedroom. And a TV and a video. The altar's on its way.

BHO: Do you ever pray?

E17 Tony: Yes, I pray daily.

BHO: And what happens?

E17 Tony: Nothing really! No lightnin' in the sky or nothin'.

BHO: Are you going to heaven, and whats it like?

E17 Tony: Haven't been there yet, not that I can remember, not in this life. Yeah, I'm going to heaven. Not going to hell.

BHO: What does God look like?

E17 Tony: The finite cannot describe the infinite.

BHO: Who's the holiest person you've ever met.

E17 Tony: You Simon.

BHO: Bless you. What music would you like at your funeral?

E17 Tony: Erm, Purple Rain – Prince.

BHO: Does the devil have all the good tunes?

E17 Tony: No. Heaven's got the best choir.

BHO: When you're on stage and being worshipped, is that a religious experience for your fans?

E17 Tony: No, not at all.

BHO: And the final question. Who would you rather have a meal with – Cliff, the Pope, Thora Hird, Harry Secombe or David Icke?

E17 Tony: Cliff. Cliff Richard. Cliff-tastic, because he's been in the business a long while and we could do a song together after the meal.

God not only plays dice. He also sometimes throws them where they cannot be seen.

Stephen Hawking, scientist.

IN TERMS OF ORGANISED RELIGION, IT'S WAFFLE AND FEEBLENESS, THAT SEEM TO GET THE FUNNIEST RESPONSE.

Ian Hislop Editor of Private Eye

BHO: The reason I played that song there ('If you don't believe in God') is that you wrote the lyrics to that tune and you were a Spitting Image scriptwriter for quite a while.

Heretic Yes, I left about five years ago but in the early years I was there quite a lot. The idea with that was that people say that the devil has all the best tunes but it struck me that he didn't really. I mean gospel music has most of them so we had this silly idea of a Tabernacle Choir that went round telling people that there wasn't a Promised Land and that they should not clap their hands or not rejoice and basically pack it in really 'cause death is all there is. Which struck me as a funny idea.

BHO: Spitting Image enjoys getting into trouble but they did have a Jesus puppet made and there was a big furore as to whether they would ever use a Mohammed puppet. They said they would but they never actually got round to doing it.

Heretic Mmm, funny that wasn't it. No I can't help thinking that when it came to offending religious minorities they didn't mind the Christians too much but with the Muslims, they thought they'd give it a miss. It wasn't a Jesus puppet anyway. I think it was an old Mike Rutherford puppet that they'd put a moustache on. I was very offended because the sketch was so un-funny, but that's just me.

BHO: So you think there are different rules for different faiths ... you can actually take the mick quite happily out of Christianity and the person of Christ, but not out of Mohammed?

Heretic Ian Hislop

I CAN'T HELP THINKING THAT WHEN IT CAME TO OFFENDING RELIGIOUS MINORITIES, SPITTING IMAGE DIDN'T MIND THE CHRISTIANS TOO MUCH, BUT THE MUSLIMS, THEY THOUGHT THEY'D GIVE IT A MISS. HMM, FUNNY THAT.

'I WANT...'

A: I want to work for peace and justice...

B: I want to stain some windows...

C: I want to wear a frock ...

A: I want to get to know people, be part of the community...

B: I want to arrange flowers every Saturday ...

C: I want to play the guitar very badly ...

A: I want to talk to God

B: I want to be quiet...

C: I want to have a bishop...

MVO: Whatever you want from life, be with the Church of England.

Heretic: Well, I'm not keen on taking the rise out of the person of Christ anyway. I think that's where you draw the line. Institutions, vicars, bishops who go a-wandering, you name it, I'm all for all that, but the central person of any faith I'm always a bit sticky about that.

BHO: You were talking on the radio the other day about a charismatic revival that took place in your school. Were you a part of that?

Heretic Oh yes, absolutely. There was a massive, full, hand-clapping evangelical renewal I suppose you'd call it, which swept through a traditional public school, which had absolutely no idea what to do about it. It was absolutely bizarre and a very exciting time, because it was certainly better than worrying about whether you were going to play for the Colts and exactly which Latin 'O' levels you were up for. But it died out sadly.

BHO: It's quite interesting because most people would expect the editor of Private Eye to be quite happy to say, 'Well anything goes, we can throw muck at anything and it really doesn't matter,' so to hear you defending Christianity or faith, might sound slightly odd.

Heretic: I'm sure it sounds very odd but I think that the essential misconception about a lot of satire is that anything goes – that you have a go at anything and you'll find that we don't. People don't have a go at anything. The whole point of using humour to make either political points or general points is that you believe in something else. I mean there's no point in saying, 'He's a crook, that's wrong, it should be done differently,' if you don't think it

matters how it is done. So, yes, *The Eye* is terrifically negative but the idea is to knock it down because you think something better should be put in it's place, not merely that you think you should knock everything down.

BHO: Is there anything in particular about organised religion that you or *Private Eye* are specifically trying to knock? Is there anything that you really think is a complete waste of time?

Heretic: I think it's the old satirical targets of 'humbug'. *Private Eye* has this joke character called the Reverend JC Flannel, and Flannel comes on and his view on everything is 'on the one hand ... and then on the other', which is the classic C of E vicar, who has no real point of view but just tells you that there are a lot of arguments and we've all really got to concentrate on this one very hard and then that's it. I think it's waffle and feebleness, in terms of organised religion, that seem to get the funniest response really. And I suppose it's in the debate about the ordination of women – two sets of hysterical opponents. On one side you had these absurd strident deaconesses and on the other side a lot of effette Anglo-Catholics swinging incense sensors and handbags and getting terribly upset at the idea of women near anything. There's good farce in the C of E at the moment.

BHO: Good farce anywhere else?

Heretic Erm ... Catholics not up to much really apart from the usual helping the third world out by telling them they can't use contraception. That goes on, a lot of that.

BHO: Baptists? Buddhists?

Heretic Haven't seen a lot of Buddhist farce. I suppose there's the Hindu revivalists in India that would be fairly farcical if it wasn't so tragic. There's Muslim fundamentalists which I suppose go beyond a joke in the Salman case.

BHO: Judaism?

Heretic Well yes, you get into immediate trouble if you criticise even the State of Israel let alone the religion of the state. We run a sort of fake Old Testament called the Book of Rabin – used to be called the Book of Shami – in which the people of Shamir go out into the desert and start smiting! And this is considered to be in bad taste. Which of course it damn well is!

BHO: Are you happy to be blasphemous?

Heretic Well I'm often accused of being blasphemous. I put a Breugel picture on the front of the Christmas issue which was called 'The Adoration of the Magi,' and we changed it to 'The Adoration of the Major,' and just put Maggie as the Madonna and this child in it's underpants as the child. A lot of people thought it was offensive. But I have to defend it saying the Christianity in that is a means of attacking the politicians, it's not the target of attack. So I'm not very happy with blasphemy generally. I suppose that where I do differ from some people is because I'm not an anarchist, I don't think anything goes.

BHO: Well you're not an anarchist Ian Hislop, but you certainly have been heretic of the week and you get to choose your favourite method of torture – so what would that be?

Heretic I suppose it would be Robert Maxwell reappearing saying 'I'm not dead at all,' and then reading out a series of writs as he handed them back to me.

BHO: Sounds fairly tortuous, we'll try and arrange it.

THE CLASSIC C OF E VICAR HAS NO REAL POINT OF VIEW BUT JUST TELLS YOU THAT THERE ARE A LOT OF ARGUMENTS AND WE'VE ALL REALLY GOT TO CONCENTRATE ON THIS ONE VERY HARD.

Strange But True

Visiting in his parish one day, a clergyman knocked at the door of one church member but got no reply. He was annoyed because he could hear footsteps and knew that the mother of the family was there. He left his visiting card, writing on it, 'Revelation 3:20 "Behold I stand at the door and knock; if anyone hears my voice and opens the door I will come to him." The next Sunday, as the parishioners filed out of church after the service, the woman who had refused to open the door handed the vicar her card with 'Genesis 3:10' written on it. Later, he looked up the passage, ' I heard the sound of thee in the garden and was afraid, because I was naked and I hid myself.'
Rev William Hinson

'BLAME GOD'

MUSIC: KLEENEX TYPE MUSIC UNDER

ANDY: ... Yeah, I blame God for the 6 million Jews who died in the holocaust. And yes, I blame God for the starving millions across the world, what's he up to? I blame him for the wars and fighting, and the suffering and for the way Mandy stormed out on me last night ... I mean, there was absolutely no need. Alright ... so I lied to her, but ... for God's sake...!

ANNOUNCER: Blame God for everything. One of life's little comforts.

hristmas

is obviously a big and holy occasion.

There have been two three-hour Big Holy

Christmas specials broadcast on One FM

It was Lord Reith – yes great relative of one of the producers of The Big Holy One – who first had the idea of The Queen's Speech, but when he asked George Vth in 1923, the King refused. But by 1923, when the Empire Service – later the World Service – was inaugurated, so that the King could speak to all his subjects over the world at once, he agreed to doing a Christmas talk. Rudyard Kipling wrote the first one in 1932.

Of course Jesus wasn't born on Christmas Day. The New Testament doesn't say too much about the details of his birth at all – only two of the four Gospels bother to mention it. But in the fourth century one of the early Popes, Julius 1st, had the idea that combining a celebration of Jesus' birthday with the great midwinter pagan festival might get the punters to fill the pews by the back door.
December 25th was chosen – how was Pope Julius to know it was also the birthday of Kenny Everett and Little Richard ?

The Queen receives up to 1,300 cards and presents from members of her public each year. She doesn't send that many ... well there's the honours system.

Such is the anger of some churchmen at the growing popularity of Santa – as opposed to Jesus – at Christmas, that in the 1950's groups of French churchmen used to get together at Christmas to burn effigies of poor Santa. Better than burning the turkey I suppose.

Contrary to what you might think, the word 'Xmas' is not a cheapy, modern shorthand for the word 'Christmas'. 'Xmas' wasn't invented because people were too lazy to spell out 'Christmas' in full. The phrase 'Xmas' has been in use for 600 years and refers to the Greek letter 'chi', the first letter of Christos, which is Greek for Christ.

Seen on a noticeboard at a church in North London:

A God Is For Life – Not Just for Christmas

THE BLESSED VIRGIN

A: Christmas …

B: … yes I love it …

A: Christmas … is so … magical …

B: … so mysterious …

A: … Yes … a mystical flight of fancy, involving the blessèd … er …

B: … the blessèd …

A: … the blessèd …

B: … the blessèd virgin.

A: Yeah. The blessèd virgin … er … airlines.

B: Virgin Airlines? Oh, well! If you want to be transported at Christmas in a full, mystical sense, transcending this temporal world I'd go straight for the … er … blessèd …

A: … blessèd …

B: … the blessèd …

A: … the blessèd …

B: … the blessèd virgin …

A: … the blessèd virgin …

B: … blessèd virgin … er … vodka.

A: Oh yeah, definitely.

B: Course Christmas could possibly be all about the blessèd virgin …

A: … the blessèd virgin …

B: … the blessèd virgin radio. But we don't believe in that anymore do we …?

A: … nah … virgin radio. Been disproved.

B: Virgin on the ridiculous …

Announcer: Good Old Blessèd Virgin. Not just there for the boring things in life like the Incarnation, but also for making loadsamoney at Christmas.

The Nativity Infant Jesus Doll

As part of a pre-Christmas awareness campaign to put the real meaning of Christmas back into childrens lives, we are offering our nativity Infant Jesus Doll at just $9.95.

The Christmas Miracle of Birth: Wrapped in Biblical swaddling clothes, this precious **INFANT JESUS DOLL** is approximatedly 18 inches long – the same size as a real newborn. True to life, as in the Divine Miracle of Birth ,the Infant Jesus Doll has 'a sweet, serene, lovable look of every newborn baby'.

Yes what a wonderful way to introduce Jesus into your child's life.

Because a warm bonding relationship is most certain to develop as your child rocks, nurtures and loves this precious infant Jesus doll. Truly a joy, an inspiration and a loving companion for children as young as two.

The Infant Jesus Doll – Because there's more to Christmas than just Santa Claus.

Big Holy Chart

The Top Five Truly Naff Records Played on the Radio in Christmas week

In at five, it's a song with the strangest theology in the world, with the possible exception of David Koresh … it's Chris de Burgh and, 'A Spaceman Came Travelling'. Down at four this week it's that marvellous seasonal evergreen, which trendy church choirs will be singing all over Christmas to 'reach the kids', 'Mary's Boy Child' by Boney M.

Up fifty places at three, an irreplaceable flares-and-sideburns seventies classic, 'So Here It Is Merry Christmas' from Slade but down at two it's Bing Crosby's pre-global-warming anthem, White Christmas.

But at number one for the second millenium running, the naffest Christmas record being played on the radio this week is the same one that was a hit in the very first Year of Our Lord, yes it's that truly dreadful pile of old sentimental tosh, Johnny Mathis's When A Child Is Born.

NASAL NATIVITY

ANNCR: Have you ever thought of a nose job?

Transport your family and friends to Bethlehem right now with new scratch 'n' sniff Christmas cards.

The Wise Men!

SFX:SCRATCHING

FVO1: Just smell that Frankincense!

FVO2: MMMmm, and that Myrrh!

MAN: Would you call this a gold card?

ANNCR: There's the scratch 'n' sniff Stable Scene …

SFX:SCRATCHING

FVO1: Mmm, that hay!

FVO2: Oooh, Joseph's aftershave!

MAN: Pfwwrrr! Real camel's breath!

ANNCR: Make this a Christmas A truly Nasal Nativity with scratch 'n' sniff cards. Available in packets of three from any religious gift shop.

Special Christmas Television Pull-out

C4 ANNCR: ... and just to remind you that at eleven o'clock this evening on Channel Four there's another chance to see, 'It Never Happened, Basically' – a contemporary look at the Christmas story by a former priest now trying to get himself a life in the media. In it, he revisits many of the original Holy Land sites, and dumps on them all. In getting back to the original masterpiece, he not only cleans away the dust, he removes the paint, puts his fist through the canvas, smashes the frame and burns the lot beyond recognition. So, that's tonight at eleven, a rather sad and damaged man presents 'It Never Happened, Basically'.

Oh, and happy Christmas from all here at Channel Four ...

A: Happy ... mas, Bill.
B: Yes, happy ... mas to you. And how are you enjoying it in

Channel Four factual programmes?
A: Oh fine, it's great.
B: Going, anywhere over ... mas?
A: No, just at home, hoping for a white ... mas for the kids.
B: Look, have you seen this seasonal Chris ... topher Columbus film ... aha! Nearly had you there ...
A: Jesus, I very nearly thought you were going to say, well, you know, the word we can't say at Channel Four.
B: Christ, no. Don't be so stupid.
ANNCR: C ... mas on Channel Four.
The Greatest Story Never Told.

CONTROLLER: What are we scheduling for Channel Four Christmas 1999, Samantha?
SAMANTHA: Well, Mike, we've done Black Christmas, Monster Raving Looney Christmas ...
CONT: ... and the Gay Christmas ...
SAM: ... and the Severely Disabled Christmas ...
CONT: ... Yes, and the Lesbian Christmas and the Single Mothers Christmas ...
SAM: ... and the Deaf Christmas ...
CONT: ... and the Vegetarian Christmas ...
SAM: ... but what about something more seasonal, more festive ...
CONT: ... Well, we could always do something with Dolphins ...
SAM: Dolphin Christmas, that's

nice ... minority group ... yes ... important and intelligent part of the audience too, yes ...
CONT: ... then there's the Liberal Democrat Christmas, they often get forgotten ...
SAM: ... Who? ...
CONT: ... But we could always go really radical and do what we've never done before ...
SAM: I like it yes ... yes ...
CONT: What about a Christian Christmas ...?
SAM: Oh don't be ridiculous ... we'd have every minority group down on us like a ton of Fatwahs.
ANNCR: Christmas on Channel Four. The Greatest Story Never Told.

NOSTALGIC
WOMAN 1: It's sad isn't it?
WOMAN 2: Yeah ... What is?
WOMAN 1: Christmas.
WOMAN 2: Yeah ... What do you mean?
WOMAN 1: It's sad when the kids stop believing in it all ...
WOMAN 2: Yeah, I mean, my Jamie, he's only eight, but today he said to me, he said 'You know Mum, I don't think I believe in all those mobile phone ads any longer ...'
WOMAN 1: It's a shame isn't it?
WOMAN 2: Yeah, 'cos you've got to believe in Christmas really haven't you ... otherwise it doesn't really work, does it ...?
WOMAN 1: Oh, no ... yes ...
ANNCR: Christmas on ITV. You have to see it to believe it. And then you won't believe it.

Big Holy Chart

The Top Five Curious First Lines of Christmas Carols

In at five this week it's 'O Little Town of Bethlehem how still we see thee lie' ... well, they must have run out of ammunition but up at four it's 'Ding Dong! Merily on high, in heaven the bells are ringing' ... then perhaps I could go to hell please, I've got a headache.

Straight in at three it's that old standard, 'We Three Kings of Orient Are' ... if the Orient weren't a rather bad football team, this might be quite a good first line. As it is, 'We eleven turkeys of Orient are ... 'might be more appropriate.

At two, down fifteen places, it's 'Once In Royal David's City, stood a lowly cattle shed' ... all part of King Herod's 'homeless in Bethlehem' social initiative. How very very caring ...

But at number one this week in the Top Five Most Curious First Lines of Christmas Carols it's 'On the first day of Christmas, my true love sent to me a partridge in a pear tree' ... er ... something tells me that my true love doesn't love me very much ...

Actress *'Jesus was born in a stable and you live in a palace… comfortably'*

In December 1993 The Big Holy One persuaded the most controversial Bishop of recent times to have a quiet Christmas chat with the woman who used to be leather-clad and Peel and opposite Steed. She is now one of the best-known actresses in the country.

The Rt Rev David Jenkins, Bishop of Durham and Diana Rigg got on very well. Unfortunately our transcript of the proceedings does not really capture the peculiarly sensual tone of voice and seductive style of delivery of the encounter. Ms Rigg was pretty attractive too.

Bishop **'On the whole as comfortably as we can given the extent of the central heating that is required to keep us warm'**

Actress: Bishop, the first question I want to ask you is about belief: there's a great parallel between the theatre and the Church. People go to the theatre in order to believe, and I as an actress have to sustain that belief. If, for a moment, I hint that I don't approve of the character I am playing or of the sentiments of the script, then I am breaking a code of some kind. You in the past have intimated that there are aspects of your script – the Bible – which you don't entirely believe in.

Bishop: Yes, but the Bible isn't really the fixed script. It's a mixture of stage directions and life-directions and responding to other people's stories by which you are supposed to live. So my script is to try and speak out as a pilgrim, believer, searcher and a person who believes I have been touched by God so that the story can go on. It isn't quite the same but it certainly involves a good deal of acting.

Actress: It certainly does but at Christmastime there are many things which are

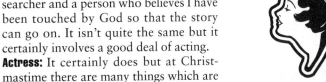

Actress *If, for a moment, I hint that I don't approve of the character I am playing or of the sentiments of the script, then I am breaking a code of some kind. You in the past have intimated that there are aspects of your script — the Bible — which you don't entirely believe in.*

adjuncts to belief – do you approve of these or not?

Bishop: Oh, I take them as they come, I think the very important thing is to enter into the spirit of the story and one of the things about Christmas cards and sometimes the way in which angels are played and so on, is to miss the spirit of the story. Because the Bible stories are immensely down to earth in a difficult Palestine where the people are worried about the future, the occupation, about the Roman soldiers, about politics and so on, and there are echoes in the stories which we have taken off and turned into something rather tinselly.

Actress: But you must have a great difficulty over Christmas because you don't believe in the Virgin Birth.

Bishop: I believe absolutely what the Virgin Birth stands for, which is that Jesus is the man God chose to become ... and I'm only agnostic about the way he did it. The story is quite clear, it is about Emmanuel – God with us – so I don't

have a problem. Especially as I myself, being a bit of an actor and I'd like to be a bit of a poet, believe that stories don't have to be literally true to get the wonder over...

Actress: No, but you can in fact make a leap of faith.

Bishop: You can make a leap of faith but if you make a leap of faith which depends on what you might call the genetic arrangements you'll be pinning faith down again. What you have to do is to get into the spirit of the story, follow this indication of God in Jesus, and see where you get, and get on from the birth story to the life and the death and the rising again story ...

Actress: I wonder. It seems to me to be rather scrubbing around the once-upon-a-time element of this story

Bishop: Well, the point about it is that it happened in time so it is once in time but it is not once upon a time, it is for now and for ever ...

Actress: People tend to go to Church at Christmas rather more than they tend to

do at other times of the year. You must find this rather depressing?

Bishop: No I'm delighted if anyone will come anywhere near the sound of the story – the story about God being so down to earth that he is quite prepared to be a baby, the story of men sitting in a field doing their job and hearing voices which are angels from heaven, the story of magicians really – not wise men – from far away who say, 'There's the star, that's the clue, let's follow it.' It's a very exciting story.

Actress: What aspects of your faith have changed since your boyhood in Bromley?

Bishop: I think, the truth is, practically nothing. The excitement of being caught up and his being interested in me so that I can be interested in Him and in the whole world, for instance, has never left me. The excitement of rummaging about in the Bible to get exciting things out of it has never left me. What has changed is that it has got broader and broader, deeper and deeper and therefore you have to be quieter and quieter about it...

Actress: Oh, really? Because in the last years of your Bishopric or hood you have in fact spoken out a great deal.

Bishop: Yes, but you speak out to things in the world out of the basis of faith, and at the heart of faith is an increasing silence into the depth of God and a silence too in one's heart about the way there are no easy answers to suffering and so on ... you just want to be alongside people rather than just dish out easy answers. What you're really attacking I think is the way in which people don't go into the depths of things but write one another off rather too easily, get caught up in trivial and not very exciting things and don't have really good enough parties...

Actress: Speaking about the silence, do you talk to God ?

Bishop: I mostly these days just sit and wait.

Actress: Do you?

Bishop: Yes, and see what pops up.

Actress: Really. You don't try and engineer ... because you have a hotline...

Bishop: Oh, course I don't, as you know ...

MUSIC:INTENSE HARDCORE JUNGLE UNDER

WIDE BOY: Coming at yer this December – Crimbo Mania!

Seven days of non-stop excess.

Yes! We've got food-mania, drink-mania, gift-mania, and now overdose on television-mania ...

Argue with your family, argue with your mates, get drunk and argue with yourself ...

We've got every combination ... all yer favourites plus loads of stuff yer didn't want and'll end up at Oxfam and they don't want either ...

The beats don't stop and neither does the divorce rate.

Chrimbo Mania – it's wicked!

Bishop **My script is to try and speak out as a pilgrim, believer, searcher and a person who believes I have been touched by God so that the story can go on.**

Big Holy Chart

Top Five Reasons To Avoid The Crib Service This Christmas

Down at five it's Mary, being played by that nasty little girl who got you with 'Trick or Treat' in November.

Up six at four it's the star fell on your head last year, guiding you only to Casualty but down eight at three in this week's top five reasons to avoid the Christmas Crib Service, it's the wise men have got flu, but still insist on sharing the gift with everyone anyway.

At two it's your son, who is always one of the sheep, despite the director's annual promises that next year it will be different. Honestly, no really. (Your son is now 19.) But straight in at number one in the top five reasons to avoid the Christmas crib service it's the worrying possibility that you might receive an annoying reminder that there's more to Christmas than the four-pack and shouting at people a lot when they stand in front of the telly. (Happy Christmas).

Actress: Just teasing …

Bishop: Everyone has as straight a line as everyone else and I think its more and more casting oneself on God and seeing what he will come up with …

Actress: Waiting …

Bishop: Yes.

Actress: If Jesus were to give the Queens Speech this year – what a wonderful opportunity that would be – what do you think he would say. Or what would you like him to say …

Bishop: I think I would hope he would say, or expect him to say, 'Look at the mess you're making of society and the world – wake up and start loving one another. When you see something wrong don't say you can't do anything about it, find someone else who thinks its wrong and start doing something about it.

Actress: And loving one another is just that …

Bishop: No, its much deeper, its putting up with one another. When you're so cross with someone that you can't stand them go and look in a mirror and see why people can't stand one another … and that is to say you've got to be ready to change yourselves and be quite as ready to find yourselves in the wrong as someone else.

Actress: Jesus was born in a stable and you live in a palace … comfortably.

Bishop: On the whole as comfortably as we can given the extent of the central heating that is required to keep us warm … yes, one has to be aware of this contrast because the Church has got involved in society in a big way and it often leads us astray. That's why you have to get back to waiting on God, looking for simplicity, using any power you've got by living in a palace to speak up for the people who are poor and left out …

Actress: I love the aspect of togetherness in church which is the hymn-singing, I sometimes drop out of a verse simply to listen to these raised human voices…and of course, Christmas is very much carols, which I love … which is your favourite carol?

Bishop: A mixture of 'Silent Night' and 'Hark The Herald Angels Sing'…

Actress: You are a very ornery Bishop … a mixture, I ask you … they're two perfect carols, why would you want to mix them?

Bishop: Well, I wouldn't, would I? I was trying to show two aspects of it. The quietness of it in 'Silent Night' and the excitement in 'Hark The Herald Angels Sing'.

Actress: In the end, for us the person in the street, what is the meaning of Christmas?

Bishop: That life has a meaning which is far deeper than we've yet guessed, that there is a power around called God who can give us promises, possibilities and newness we can't possibly imagine and therefore we should simply enjoy Christmas and not be afraid that the spirit of Christmas will go away in the New Year.

Actress: Thank you very much Bishop and Happy Christmas.

Bishop: Happy Christmas.

SAINSBURY RECIPE

MUSIC:CLASSICAL MUSIC

VO: For the ultimate Christmas, just follow this recipe …

Take four weeks wages and spread evenly on presents, making sure to spend less than you receive … then add extended family.

Place in front room and leave to boil over for three long days.

Mix in: too much rich food, rows over the James bond film plus a handful of snide comments until bitter. While the temperature is still too hot, pour in some alcohol.

Add some more alcohol.

And some more.

And finish the bottle.

Once completely tanked, drop in some unnecessary abuse, and leave simmering.

Repeat until the excitement, fun and good humour has completely evaporated.

And that's my recipe for disaster.

DOSS

SFX:SUPERMARKET ATMOS

BAKER: Hello there. Danny Baker calling. Cheeky banter, cheeky banter. Excuse me madam – what's your name?

WOMAN: Charlotte Smith

BAKER: Magic. Apples and pears. Cockney humour. Tell me, Mrs Smith, would you swap your Regular Christmas Doss in front of the telly for Old Traditional Christmas at church with carol singing?

WOMAN: You must be joking …

BAKER: Thought not. Cheeky chuckle.

This Christmas, stick with 'Doss'. Now with 100% apathy.

Big Holy Chart

Top Five Modern Christmas Traditions

In at five it's the publication, several months early, of the Christmas issue of the Radio Times. After all television is the real meaning of Christmas …

At two this week it's unhappy families, as all those families who get together for Christmas are rudely reminded of why they don't get together the other 364 days of the year …

Up seven hundred places at three in this week's top modern Christmas traditions, it's the Government's multi-million pound Christmas anti-drink-drive advertising campaign … every television advert swiftly followed by another one telling you what to drink all over Christmas…

Down at four this week it's anti-hunt campaigners joining forces with anti-vivisectionists, vegans and vegetarians to launch pre-Christmas assaults on Britain's turkey farms in an aim to liberate all the fat, oppressed occupants … gobble, gobble, gobble … but at number one it's the nation's free-thinking chain-stores and supermarkets, deciding to open all day on Christmas Day so that every one, everywhere has a real choice of when they shop… and no one can Keep Christmas Day Special anymore.

'MISSING'

ANNCR: [SERIOUS] And now a Christmas appeal from Joe and Mary …

MARY: Hello, I'm Mary and we want to ask if you've seen my son.

JOSEPH: Yeah. Hi, I'm Joseph we seem to have lost our boy …

MARY: Well, my boy actually …

JOSEPH: … if you know where our boy is we'd like you to …

MARY: … well my boy actually …

JOSEPH: … whatever … your boy … our boy … the thing is it's his birthday on Christmas Day and what with all the eating and drinking and TV and that, he must have got forgotten …

MARY: … 'Cos he's nowhere to be seen. I just want my boy back …

JOSEPH: … our boy …

MARY: … whatever … for a happy birthday …

JOSEPH: … and a happy Christmas … if you know what I mean …

MARY: … we mean …

ANNCR: Let's get this stable family back together this Christmas.

ALCO-DRIP

ANNCR: Be romantic at the Christmas party …

DRUNK 1: Y'know, I always fancied you darlin' [HIC]

ANNCR: Be witty at family gatherings …

DRUNK 2: Aw, sod off Auntie …

ANNCR: With new Alco-Drip. The handy strap-on pouch drip-feeds the booze straight into your bloodstream ….

DRUNK 1: Another pint of Creme de Menth, my good man …

ANNCR: Wear it under your party best for hands-free Christmas cheer – the seasonal spirit on tap! So you can be the life and soul of the party …

DRUNK 1: I think I'm gonna be sick …

DRUNK 2: I just have been …

ANNCR: Alco-Drip. Refreshes the Paralitics that overdrinking fails to reach.

'PRUDENTIAL'

MUSIC:GENTLE MUSIC UNDER

WIFE: I want a quiet Christmas – at home with my family …

BOY: I want loads and loads of presents and chocolate and crisps and lemonade …

GIRL: I want to go somewhere hot and sunny …

LAD: I wanna get lagered with me mates every single night

OAP: I want to decorate the house with tinsel, and holly, and shiny baubles …

WOMAN: I want someone to remember what Christmas is really about …

VO: Whatever you're looking for this Christmas, you're bound to get a cheap pair of orange socks from your Gran. You always do. [PAUSE] Annoying isn't it?

LIPOSUCTION

FVO: Tuck and suck. [BURP]

- Eat as much as you like this Christmas without gaining an ounce. [BURP]

- Tuck in. Suck out.

- As you put on the pounds we'll take them off [BURP] in comfort with our new Lardass Liposuction Mobile Flab Laboratory. [BURP]

- You stay at home eating and our reps come with their tubes and suck out the flab as you suck it in. [BURP]

- Tuck in – without a care in the world – to your 28th helping of christmas pudding with brandy butter and rum sauce [BURP] and watch the calories flow out through our smart transparent tubes into our smart transparent bucket. [BURP]

- Tuck and suck. Book now and get a 30% discount. [BURP]

- Call freefone Tuck and Suck now, and get a 30% reduction on your reduction with our suction.

Big Holy Chart

Top Five Reasons Not To Go Back To Church After Christmas

In at five it's the church's heating system which is obviously based on the carol, "In the bleak midwinter…'
At four it's a new entry, the only thing more lukewarm than the welcome you get is the coffee afterwards
Up at three this week is the troubling realisation that the verger is more ugly than the gargoyle.
At two, it's no change this week, for the pipes are as frozen up as the vicar's emotional life.
And straight in at number one in the top five reasons not to go back to church after Christmas it's the curate who will again be preaching on his new year resolutions about tithing (yours not his). God save us all.

The Big Holy Guide to

The Children of God

The Children of God were founded in 1968 by American David Brandt Berg after he prophecied that an earthquake would plunge California into the sea and he – 'Moses' – would rescue God's children.

The Children have a sexy reputation, fostered by the founder: 'We have a sexy god and a sexy religion and a very sexy leader with a very sexy following', Berg once wrote.

Many women followers were expected to get out on the streets and become 'hookers for Jesus' – to attract new converts. Berg called this F-F – Flirty Fishing.

At one time 'Chairman Mo' claimed to have several spiritual counsellors including the Pied Piper, Joan of Arc, Oliver Cromwell and Merlin the Magician.

Children of God, perhaps only 12,000 strong these days, believe the world-system of government is inspired by the Devil and that Armageddon will take place when Russia invades Israel.

Moses, who said Jesus would return in 1993, still wrote to his followers until his death in 1994 – but they had to write back through a PO Box in Switzerland. He was in hiding in the Far East.

You can't meet God's gift to women in a singles' bar.

If the singles life sometimes leave you feeling alone and empty, remember that God's gift to all women and men is Jesus Christ. Come join us in worship this Sunday at Family Worship Centre.

Family Worship Centre

ntre — Corner of 106 Ave. & 96 St. 424-6422

An electricity worker in Guyana, Ray Charles, who was convicted of assaulting a colleague in a scuffle, was given the option of singing a hymn or facing some other kind of punishment. A magistrate in Georgetown, K Juman-Yasin, told Charles that he ought to have some singing talent because he had the same name as the American rhythmn and blues singer. The 26-year old then gave an off-key rendition of 'In The Name of Jesus, We Have the Victory'. After a standing ovation from spectators he gave an encore and the magistrate discharged him with a reprimand.

Strange But True

CHEAP CONFESSION

A Franciscan friar in Massachusetts is handing out coupons to Roman Catholics who confess their sins which give them 50% off their penance. Rev Bede Ferrara says he wants to avoid a 'spiritual recession'. The coupons allow a churchgoer who confesses and receives a penance of 30 Hail Mary's to only do 15. They also ask for donations of canned food to the church if possible.

Sir Jonathon Porritt

BHO: I want to get this out of the way, right at the very beginning and you know what's coming: when religion and the green movement come up, people have an image of turquoise tracksuits and you know who and the 'son of God' and so on ... shall we just get it out of the way?

Heretic: Yes let's, because it wasn't helpful then and it's not helpful even now that people think about green or spiritual matters in the context of David Icke temporarily losing his marbles. It's still damaging because a lot of people in the green movement want to stress the importance of the spiritual dimension, want to work on the spiritual dimension and find that a lot of people can't quite make that jump. They still think it's into some very weird and wacky extremist stuff.

BHO: Are you not into weird and wacky extremist stuff?

Heretic: I'm not into weird and wacky stuff at all, no. I'm a little bit into what you might describe as the fringe end of green spirituality, the sort of tree-hugging end of it.

BHO: You're into tree-hugging. This is very heretical, I love it.

Heretic: Yeah, it's quite serious this. On occasions I can commune with nature as well as the next man or woman, and indeed genuinely do derive a great sense of satisfaction out of that.

BHO: Out of hugging a tree?

Heretic: Well ... occasionally. I mean more often it's ...

BHO: What sort of a tree?

Heretic: Oh, I don't think one should be too selective about them because after all they are all manifestations of God's purpose. I do happen to be particularly into beech trees since you're pressing this point.

BHO: Right – bit of a beech tree feeler, ok.

Heretic: But my tree-hugging, it has to be said, is set in what some people would see as a much more conventional context in that I would call myself a Christian though some Christians would be very upset at the notion that there are some Christians out there hugging trees. But for me that emerges quite naturally ...

BHO: There's a lot of Christians hugging weirder things than trees it has to be said, but anyway ...

Heretic: (continuing regardless) ... that emerges quite naturally out of what you might describe as a green theology; and a green theology is not the same as a kind of all purpose-new-age pantheism where one imagines that somehow the earth itself is a god or the earth itself is holy. I don't actually feel that, I respond to the earth as part of God's purpose, as a part of God's creation.

BHO: So in what sense is your faith, Christian faith then ?

Heretic: Primarily because I do think that the earth was created. I do believe in a creator God, and I think that it's margin-

JESUS WAS A TYPICAL MAN – THEY ALWAYS SAY THEY'LL COME BACK BUT YOU NEVER SEE THEM AGAIN. Graffiti.

I'M NOT INTO WEIRD AND WACKY STUFF AT ALL, NO. I'M A LITTLE BIT INTO WHAT YOU MIGHT DESCRIBE AS THE FRINGE END OF GREEN SPIRITUALITY, THE SORT OF TREE-HUGGING END OF IT.

ally more fantastical to believe in evolution by chance as it were – ie the secular interpretation of evolution – rather than evolution by purpose, and the purposefulness of it comes from God. I mean it's a toss-up frankly, it could go either way.

BHO: Presumably Judaism would say a lot of the same kind of thing; a lot of religions would say, 'I'm with you Jonathan.'

Heretic: Indeed and I think that it is fair to say that although a lot of green Christians in every single one of the world's major religions, and what is at stake here – apart from the heretics as it were – is the extent to which those religions try and rediscover that tradition; how much do they actually emphasise what is there? It's not a question of going back and re-writing their sacred texts or anything like that because obviously no-one's into that kind of stuff. But it is a question of going back and re-interpreting what is there.

BHO: This doesn't sound very New Age and hippy which is what people often

BHO: **WHAT SORT OF A TREE?**

Heretic: **OH, I DON'T THINK ONE SHOULD BE TOO SELECTIVE ABOUT THEM BECAUSE AFTER ALL THEY ARE ALL MANIFESTATIONS OF GOD'S PURPOSE. I DO HAPPEN TO BE PARTICULARLY INTO BEECH TREES SINCE YOU'RE PRESSING THIS POINT**

would call themselves Christians they would also emphasise the ecumenical nature of what they're doing. They wouldn't deny that other people in other faiths have access to that truth – there is no sense that it is only the Christian God that provides meaning or salvation to people on planet earth. That, I think is not probably a widely held green view.

BHO: A lot of religious leaders like politicians find it cool to be green. Is true religion green or is it just an affectation? I mean the Archbishop of Canterbury is supposed to be the 'green archbishop' – is there a genuine green thrust to faith?

Heretic: There is a genuine green thread associate with the green dimension.

Heretic: Well, I have a lot of sympathy with New Age people because to a certain extent they are trying to seek part of the truth. They are trying to do it in a gentle and usually extremely inoffensive way and it really irritates the hell out of me that there are some theologians and dogmatists in the Church of England particularly, who think that the New Age movement represents the devil on earth. They seem to get more upset about the slightly muddled spiritual questing of the New Age movement than they do about the millions of people on earth who have no spiritual or religious interests whatsoever.

I do not understand how thay have this totally biased antipathy to the New Age movement.

BHO: Is there a danger of worshipping the earth as opposed to anything else?
Or might that be fine ...?

Heretic: There are still a lot of people who are into what you might call good old fashioned pantheism – worshipping the earth as a source of sacred authority in itself – worshipping trees, lakes, rivers, stones and so on as the origin of religious authority. But I don't really see earth worship itself as any kind of impediment to Christians or members of any other religious persuasions coming to a greener perspective.

BHO: A lot of people of faith are at heart hopeful people. As an environmentalist though you must be permanently depressed?

Heretic: Well I'm not actually but that may well be to do with a resource that is spiritual if you like and that's something I do call on when I get depressed. I do actually find that strengthens me as much as anything else.

BHO: Before you go you do have to choose your chosen method of torture, which we might be able to arrange; what would you like?

Heretic: Well I've thought about this as you can imagine and I think really the most painful thing for me would be to have Theresa Gorman and one or two other politicians of her ilk, lecturing me about why there are no environmental problems in the world today. I think that would very quickly persuade me to do whatever it is that you want me to do as a heretic.

People come into my house and they're most surprised at the way I live. I don't sleep upside down on rafters I don't turn into a vampire at midnight. I live quite a normal life you know.

Ozzy Osborne

BHO: We've just been listening to an item about White Metal, all these Christtians playing metal music – does it strike you as odd at all.

Heretic: I'm not a satanist, I'm not a practising churchgoer but I believe in God, I don't believe in the devil for one minute. People come into my house and they're most surprised at the way I live. I don't sleep upside down on rafters, I don't turn into a vampire at midnight. I live quite a normal life you know.

BHO: You threw liver over your audience once but this band Stryper thrown Bibles at their audience ...

Heretic: Yeah well I mean if you do believe in the Bible it's kinda sacrificial in a lot of ways.

BHO: Sacreligious.

Heretic: It's a sin to throw the holy book ... it's just as bad as me throwing liver y'know.

BHO: You said you believe in God though you don't go to church. I was reading this week a piece from the New York Times that actually you're a member of the Church of England.

Heretic: I was christened as a Protestant under the Church of England – I suppose I am a member but I'm not a practising member. In other words I don't go to church, although my children do go to a Christian school.

BHO: It also says here that you kneel and pray backstage before going on.

Heretic: Yeah I do, I say the serenity prayer every night, I have to as part of my recovery programme from my alcohol problem. "God grant me the serenity to accept the things I cannot change, the courage to change the things I can, and the wisdom to know the difference."

BHO: So you're not the anti-Christ then?

Heretic: Not at all. Vincent Price is a great actor and most of his roles have been about vampires and all the rest of it but yet in his spare time he wrote cookery books – not things like bat soup or whatever. He wrote very good cookery books. What I'm trying to say here is it's only my act, it's what they want to see of me. Like a clown in a circus – when he goes home he takes his red nose and his make up off and he's just a regular Joe Blow y'know. When you start involving religion with music, it says in the book "Beware of false prophets". You end up like the guy in Waco y'know. I'm not a religious fanatic. I just think add another 'o' to God and you've got good and that's the way I thought about myself.

The Big Holy Guide to

The Unification Church

In Seoul's Olympic Stadium, South Korea in 1992, 40,000 brides and grooms created the loudest 'I Do' in history. They were all members of the Unification Church and the minister was Sun Myung Moon their founder.

The Church was set up in 1954 by Mr Moon, now 75, who claimed that a revelation from Jesus when he was 16 told him to restore God's Kingdom. Later Buddha and Moses helped him write The Divine Principle, which Moonies claim is the latest revelation from God.

Moonies believe that when Satan seduced Eve he started an unholy trinity, that Jesus is the second Adam but because he didn't get married he didn't start the necessary holy trinity and so a new messiah is needed who is currently on his way here.

Behind the Church is the Tongil Group, a business empire with interests in publishing, property, soft drinks, universities and even armaments.

The Church has denied accusations of brainwashing converts but not that Mr Moon was sentenced to a year in an American prison in 1984 for tax-evasion.

The wedding couples, by the way, paid an average $1000 each – that's $60m to Mr Moon for a twenty minute ceremony. Nice work if you can get it.

ATHEISM

DEREK: ... Today, Dave, we celebrate the triumph of atheism across the entire world!

DAVE: I'll drink to that.

DEREK: Well, inevitable really – given what we know now ...

DAVE: (PAUSE) Apart from Islam, of course

DEREK: Sorry?

DAVE: Apart from Islam, Derek

DEREK: Oh right, the complete triumph of atheism across the world, apart from Islam.

DAVE: And ... er ... the Jewish people –

DEREK: They are indeed another major world religion still in existence, Dave – but apart from them –

DAVE: ... And, apart from a few billion Christians

DEREK: A few billion Christians, maybe

DAVE: And the large block of humanity who follow the Hindu faith –

DEREK: There is the Hindu faith to consider, undoubtedly –

DAVE: Then there's the Buddhists ...

DEREK: ... Many millions of Buddhists I'm sure, Dave. How astute.

DAVE: ... And the countless number of individuals engaged in a private search for some transcendent truth –

DEREK: Indeed Dave, but apart from Islam, Judaism, Christianity, Hinduism, Buddhism and the countless number of individuals engaged in a private search for religious truth – who else is there?

DAVE: Yeah, but ... that only leaves the Humanist Society, Derek

DEREK: (LESS SURE) Precisely, Dave, just my point – today we celebrate the triumph of atheism across the ... er ... entire Humanist Society ...

DAVE: I'll drink to that ...

BIGOT

A: I hate those Catholics. And the Muslims ... Moslems ... Muslims – don't like them at all. Or those Protestant fundamentalists. Oh, and the Hindus – don't know what they're on about ...

... and I do not like Jews. Nope. Buddhists! What do they know? And those people in orange robes make me sick as well, wandering up and down clanging their cymbals. I hate the lot of them ...

Announcer: Religious bigotry. One of life's little comforts.

The Rt Rev Michael Marshall and the completely unreverend Helen Lederer

Actress: Bishop Michael, why do Christians seem to see the sexual sins as the absolute ultimate terrible thing?

Bishop: I don't think we do if I'm really honest. If you look at the history of the church well all the mediaeval Popes … most of them were fornicators. Certainly you didn't have to resign in the middle ages if you were in office in government or the church just for the peccadillo or the sin of fornication. That's been imposed upon us by a so called liberal society as a matter of fact. When the church was in control – if you look in the age of Chaucer and Canterbury Tales and all the rest of it – I mean they were a pretty randy lot. A lot of fun.

Actress: Well that's true because that taps into the Catholic idea particularly that priests have to be celibate but then how can they share understanding and compassion about things – sex goes with relationships but if they don't experience it …

Bishop: Yes it seems to me that the Roman Catholic church recently, has certainly got sex on the brain. It's not surprising considering that all their theology about sex is done by celibate priests and bishops who, if they've had any experience about sex, jolly well shouldn't have had. We need the whole people of God; men and women to be involved in this debate about what is the proper use of sex and that's really what the church wants to do, because you know we can do a lot of damage to people through sex and I think that's what the Christian faith is trying to wean us from.

Actress: But I was thinking that although Catholics have a particular position on sex that you yourself as you say don't share …

When the Church was in control – if you look in the age of Chaucer and Canterbury Tales and all the rest of it – I mean they were a pretty randy lot.

It's relationships which are immortal or eternal. I'm very suspicious about clouds and harps ... I wouldn't feel very at home there would you?

Bishop: I certainly don't.

Actress: . . . Christians still say that sex is fine, but within marriage. I wondered what your attitude is to sex as a part of an exploratory thing in a relationship.

Bishop: The difficulty with that is that if the sexual aspect of a relationship gets up front it's very difficult to get out of that relationship without parties being wounded and hurt by that. I think it's much more important in a relationship to develop the things that you've got in common, common interests and so on to make sure there's a friendship at the root of this relationship because the sexual angle tends to get less later in life. You see I want to know if you'll love me when I'm still no good at it. 'Will you still love me when I'm sixty four,' that marvellous phrase of the Beatles. It seems to me to have to wake up every morning and say 'Now darling, am I proving this relationship's got any substance in it?' is putting a lot of pressure on both parties.

Actress: So how did the joke about the Actress and the Bishop actually start?

Bishop: I think it originated in that time when people realised that the theatre and the church have a great deal in common. When I had a parish in the West End I used to visit many of the theatres, Raymond's Revue Bar and so on.

Actress: Oh my God.

Bishop: No, no, no, it was a marvellous relationship of tremendous honesty actually and I think that earlier societies realised that bishops were also somewhat controversial figures and there's a real bonding between the acting world and the church at it's best.

Actress: And of course they both wear frocks if you'll forgive my cheekiness.

Bishop: I don't mind that at all.

Actress: Now Bishop I recently went to that film called 'Alive', which was a true story – a plane crash where people were forced to eat their own dead after they'd crashed and they were on their last legs, if you'll excuse the dreadful pun, when they were rescued. Obviousy they had to look at death there as a reality. They must have thought 'So what's next'? They must have had to think about heaven. What is heaven like? Is it nice?

Bishop: The answer is I have to honestly say 'I don't know' and I don't need to know. But what I do know which is much more important is, the person I'm coming to know this side of death – Christ – will also be there the other side and that relationship with him will continue. It's relationships which are immortal or eternal. I'm very suspicious about clouds and harps ... I wouldn't feel very at home there would you?

Actress: I'd probably feel very distracted and want to start learning how to play and things. So you don't bog yourself down then with imagining how you would spend your time in this place called heaven.

Bishop: No I don't. Any more than if suppose you were going to go and live in bongo-bongo land and you were frightfully worried because you didn't know the language or how they dress or what they eat. Well if I said, 'That's alright, Helen, as a matter of fact I've got a very good friend who lives in bongo-bongo

land – I'll ask them to meet you the minute you get off the aircraft. You don't need to know any of these other details because they'll take care of all that. Now that's exactly the Christian approach to the unknown of death. This world is just a courtship and the next world is the real thing.

Actress: You know it will be a nice place if you lived a reasonably good life on earth?

Bishop: It will be as good as life on this earth has been for you. D'you see what I mean. It'll pick up the other side of the grave where you left off ... hell is an eternal possibility which we always are free to choose – sometimes we choose not to go to the party but just to stay outside. But actually, at the end of the day, I don't think anybody will actually go there.

Actress: But you are an Anglican – a lot of the more extreme groups will say that hell is very prominent in their picture of things.

Bishop: Yes and some people use hell as a kind of cane to beat people over the head and make them believe. Now you can't do that – belief is trust, you can't make me trust you. I don't know if you saw the film 'Flatliners' but it seems to me that was part of a morbid curiosity with the geography and the furniture and fittings of what it's like on the other side. I don't want to know that. What I want to know is that the one who I'm coming to know now – ie God – will be there in the next chapter of my life, and the friendship I've already begun with him will blossom and be enriched to encompass lots of other people on the other side of death.

Actress: Sounds better than life actually.

Bishop: Exactly, the line I should have said.

Strange But True

A British research organisation calculated that the population of Heaven is 5,473,000,000. It reached the heavenly roll call tally by adding up all the deaths since 40,000BC – roughly 60 billion – then figuring out the world's Christian population and doing an estimate from 8,000BC.

The whole idea of messiahs is humanity's desperation for one person to come along and solve all it's problems

David Icke

BHO: Hello David.

Heretic: Hello Simon, very pleased to be heretic of the week. It's a very honourable and sound position to be in, I feel.

BHO: One of the reasons for talking to you is to be able to ask you – in the wake of the recent Waco tragedy – what it is that pushes people out of mainstream religion and into sects like the Branch Davidian cult ?

Heretic: The horrors that we've seen in Waco are really – if you look at the history of religion and what happens around the world today – just a microcosm, a really extreme focus of what the so-called 'great' religions of the world like Roman Catholicism have been doing for centuries. They've been mind-controlling, brain-washing people, manipulating them through fear and guilt and this still goes on today. And really if we're gonna sort out the problems of this planet and sort out the problems of humanity, then we really have got to start thinking for ourselves.

People say 'Will there be another Waco ...' well, of course there will ... while there are vast numbers of people in the world who are desperate to pass on responsibility for how they think and behave to some cult or to some guru or to some church or political system.

BHO: er ...

Heretic: (in full swing) ... the time has come to ditch all that nonsense, take information from all sources but make up our own minds what we wish to believe and how we wish to behave, because in the end, we are responsible for the way we think and act and we can't pass it on to someone else which humanity is all the time desperately trying to do.

BHO: But I can hear people saying that David Koresh said he was the son of God and that's something that you said at one time.

Heretic: Now hold on a minute, you've used the word there, I never said that. I said that I was *a* – and you see I don't actually use the word God. I use 'infinite mind'.

Heretic: Well you did at one stage.

BHO: Well yeah I did, I did. The three words 'son of god ' get humanities' knickers into such a collective twist because of all the stuff with religion, that it does act

... the so called 'great' religions of the world like Roman Catholicism have been mind-control-ling, brain-wash-ing and manipu-lating people through fear and guilt for centuries

RIGHT & WRONG

DEREK: ...And I said to Barry, I said, 'Barry – there is no such thing as right and wrong these days -'

DAVE: Right

DEREK: I mean, given what we know now, you just cannot say to someone, 'You are wrong!'

DAVE: No, you're right, Derek – that is wrong

DEREK: Frankly, Dave, they are outmoded concepts – each individual must decide for themselves how to behave. We must appeal to Natural Law here, appeal to core principles, appeal to that basic and inherent sense in the human soul of that which is just, of that which is acceptable and that which is unacceptable.

DAVE: Know what we're talking about here, Derek?

DEREK: What's that?

DAVE: We're talking right and wrong, Derek.

DEREK: Precisely Dave – and we should not be afraid of those words; we should not be afraid to say to someone, 'You are wrong.'

DAVE: Right...

as an enormously effective focus, especially when you're in the public eye as I was at the time. If you want to use symbolic language then we're all a son or daughter of god because we're all an aspect of this energy, this consciousness and it just so happens that using those three little words can attract enormous amounts of interest from which you can then project what you're really saying.

We're in a fantastically exciting decade when the so called 'great mysteries' of life which have been apparently beyond humanities abilities to solve, will be revealed and they will be revealed on many fronts by psychics, by enlightened scientists and by others.

BHO: And in your book.

Heretic: Well yes. I think my autobiography for many reasons will be a little bit like dropping a nuclear device into conventional thought because I feel that the greatest gift that anyone can give to the human race is to encourage people to think and question. The most liberating word in the English is 'why?' Once you start applying the word 'why' to the present way of doing things, the present political economic, scientific and religious system, the whole house of cards crumbles before your eyes and that's going to happen for a lot of people in this decade. The days of religious dominance, conventional scientific dominance, the imposition of someone else's view upon humanity is coming to an end and I think the appropriate word that religions use is hallelujah to that!

BHO: If you say so. You've explained what you meant by 'son of God'. David Koresh said he was 'the son of God', do you think he was mad, psychotic?

Heretic: I would say very clearly that anyone who calls themself the messiah and starts quoting the scriptures to justify that, is in a very confused state because there are no messiahs.

The whole idea of messiahs is humanity's desperation for one person to come along and solve all it's problems. We all have to solve the problems of the world, we're all responsible for them, we're all responsible for the solutions. So if we're gonna hang about and wait for some messiah guy to come down on a cloud and say I'll put it all right, we're gonna wait to the end of the world. It's time for individual action and time for individuals to take responsibility for those actions and those thoughts.

BHO: There's one thing I wanted to mention. I've left it to the end in case you hang up on me. Did you hear what Jasper Carrott said about you?

Heretic: I did hear that he did quite a funny thing about it yeah.

BHO: He just said 'David Icke thinks he can save the world. He never saved anything at Coventry, why should he start now?'

Heretic: Actually when I was a goalkeeper Simon they used to call me Cinderella cause I kept missing the ball.

BHO: David Icke thank you and now you have to choose your method of torture.

Heretic: Watching Leicester City trying to get in the Premier League. .

BHO: Perhaps they should play in turquoise, Dave?

Heretic: Well if they do that they would get lots of rubbish thrown at them.

The Big Holy Guide to
Jehovahs Witnesses.

The most famous Jehovah's Witness in the world is pop-singer Michael Jackson who is said to undertake clandestine door to door work for the organisation, selling copies of their magazine The Watchtower, possibly in disguise as a black man.

The Jehovah's Witnesses were founded in 1931 by Pastor Charles Taze Russell of Pennsylvania. They teach that God is one person – Jehovah – who once existed all alone in space and created Jesus – not divine – who was originally the archangel Michael.

JW's do not celebrate birthdays, Christmas or Easter, opt out of religious education at school, refuse to take blood transfusions and refuse military service. Sometimes this has even led to the death of the JW concerned.

Members believe we are living in the last days and JW's have regularly predicted the date of the end of the world. Still, they've only got to get it right once eh?

JW's believe that governments are controlled by the devil, Armageddon will end it all and survivors will reign with Christ for 1000 years. After that a lucky 144,000 will live in heaven, and the rest will have to make do on earth. If you don't join up you will be annihilated – think about that the next time they knock on your door.

THEOLOGY

DEREK: ... And then, Dave, I discover that this geezer stood next to me with the Guinness, actually studied theology!

DAVE: Theology? Ten out of ten on the Richter scale of yawns there, Derek.

DEREK: Well, right, I mean given what we know now, just how can someone spend all day long contemplating God, Sex, Power, Death, Healing, Mysticism and Forgiveness?!

DAVE: Sad, isn't it? I mean, frankly, who but a Martian could be interested in a superhuman being having power over nature ...?

DEREK: What kind of person is interested in Sex?

DAVE: Not me, and who would bother to concern themselves with anything as trivial as Power?

DEREK: And a subject like Death. Who cares?

DAVE: Not me. And Healing. A complete waste of time.

DEREK: Mysticism and the unexplained. Per-leeease!

DAVE: Forgiveness? For God's sake!

DEREK: My point exactly, Dave.

DAVE: So did he ... er ... say where he studied it, like ... er ... an address to write to that sort of thing ...?

DEREK: Well, its funny you should say that, Dave, 'cos he left me the brochure and apparently there's a course starting next week...

DAVE: Well, If I picked you up after work ...

DEA†H

AVOIDANCE

A: Death? Don't like the word, that's all. Don't like to talk about it. I mean, I think it's morbid. 'Passed away', I prefer that. But it shouldn't be talked about at all. The whole subject's not nice …

… No it's morbid. Out of sight out of mind, that's best really. That's what I think … (FADING)

ANNOUNCER: Avoiding the subject. One of life's little comforts

Big Holy Chart

Top Five Ways to Get Your earthly self disposed of…

In the kitchen deep freezer … but if there's a power cut you might go off

Far out at sea … but you might get washed up on Eastbourne beach …

In the back- garden … but the next owners may dismember you when they're putting up the new patio.

In the local churchyard … but most of them are fuller than Tesco's multi-storey on Saturday afternoon.

Down the crematorium … but your post-barbie noxious gases will add to the greenhouse effect.

Seven Things About Halloween You May Not Know

Intrinsically

Derek: So what d'you reckon to Halloween, Derek?

Dave: An apparently simple celebration Dave involving pumpkins ... and er ... well, all things pertaining to the spooky and the ghoulish ...

Derek: I notice that you use the words 'apparently simple' implying that there is more to all this than meets the eye ...

Dave: I think we can safely say that in this matter Dave, we see only the tip of the iceberg ...

Derek: No, I've never seen those used ... turnip heads, yes...

Dave: What I am saying Dave, is that the popularity of Halloween is related in no small part to its status as a phenomenological entity with both philosophical and theological undergirdings resonating deeply with the buried human psyche.

Derek: And I suppose it's also a good excuse for a booze-up and a fancy-dress party.

Dave: Well, there is that as well, obviously, yeah ... yeah.

All Hallows Eve

Did you know? All Hallows Eve – or Halloween – was originally a pagan festival of the dead which has survived to into the 1990's as a night of trick-or-treating by children dressed up as goblins on doorsteps demanding jaffa cakes or they'll frighten your dogs.

It takes place on October 31st – obviously – and is followed – obviously again – by November 1st, which is All Hallows Day, also called All Hallowman, All Saints, All Saints Day and All Souls Day.

The ancient Celts

called this Festival Samhain (pronounced Sow'an) – which means 'end of summer' – and they used it to celebrate the arrival of winter. In Ireland the Druids sacrificed to their deities by burning victims in wickerwork cages.

The veil between the worlds of the living and the dead was believed to be at its thinnest point in the year, making communication between the living and the dead much easier. On the eve of the holiday, the souls of the dead freely roamed the land of the living – ooh, er, Mrs.

Modern celebrants of halloween

still believe that the unseen worlds of the Devil and witches have a free hand to exercise their powers tonight. Some believe that certain ceremonies can be used to foretell events, mostly about the identity and qualities of future marital partners – be they good-looking, rich, well-endowed ?

For example, if a young person eats a raw or roasted salt herring before going to bed, the future husband or wife will appear in a dream offering a drink of water. (Water? What kind of future spouse is that?)

The Milky Way

is sometimes known as The Road of the Gods or Road of the Souls, and has been regarded as a river of spirit light since ancient times. The Milky Way is also seen as milk from a womans breast or – eeeyeuch ! – as sperm from a man. This is said to tie into concepts of reincarnation ... I'd rather not, if that's alright with everyone else.

Talking about the dead, ever heard of The Bridge of Souls ?

Well, believe it or not, it's a mythical heavenly path by which the souls of the dead are said to travel to their afterlife.

Spitting Image

If you do happen to see a ghost – being as the veil is said to be lifted tonight between the dead and the living – I've got just the tip for you: a good gob.

Spitting is said to avert evil and protect against ghosts, witches and evil spirits. When one encounters a ghost, the ancient wisdom goes, one must spit on the ground in front of it and demand, 'In the name of the Lord, what do you want?'

Your spiritually-reinforced gob, according to legend, will prevent the ghost from harming anyone.

Ever been told to 'stop acting like a zombie'?

Unless you were dead and buried they probably never knew what they were telling you. In Voodoo beliefs, a zombie is a dead person allegedly restored to life by a sorcerer. The zombie has no will of its own but acts as a robot-like slave to the sorcerer – a bit like an Everton player.

Other people believe the person is dead – yes, just like an Everton player.

But according to Zombie experts

Zombies may in fact be real; although not actually resurrected dead people. The chances are they are poisoned, brain-damaged individuals who give the appearance of being dead.

One scientist, who interviewed real zombies in Haiti, was told how they had 'died' – by being administered poisons in their food or in their wounds that made them sink into a death-like coma. Once buried alive, the sorceror 'resurrected' them with another chemical mixture, beat them or starved them into submission, leaving them permanently scarred.

It is sad actually that many Christians show how holy they are by wearing the face of someone who has drunk an unexpected dose of castor oil.

Desmond Tutu

BHO: It is Halloween and all Ghosts and Ghoulies and three-legged beasties, Archbishop Desmond Tutu, is it all harmless fun?
Archbishop: I believe it is good for us to be made to enjoy religion and the things of religion, but it also does speak about unseen realities, that yes, there are spirits, bad and good.
BHO: But there are some churches for example that will not have anything to do with Halloween. They do not like the festivities that go with it, they don't like the pumpkins ... because they say it is demonic.
Archbishop: It is sad actually that many Christians show how holy they are by wearing the face of someone who has drunk an unexpected dose of castor oil. Why do they think that glumness necessarily says anything about holiness.
BHO: So you don't have a problem. If I invite you to a Halloween party, you'd go.
Archbishop: I'd go, yes. Why not? I'd dress up.

BHO: Well you dress up for your job...
Archbishop: We are always dressing up, I mean we are always acting, it is part of a great drama this business of being human, it is great fun...
BHO: Do you think there are ghosts?
Archbishop: There may be.
BHO: You haven't seen one ever?
Archbishop: I don't think I have yet.
BHO: Would it be a theological problem if you saw one?
Archbishop: I don't think necessarily, no. I don't think that we ought to make out that we know more than we know. Why God complained against the friends of Job was that he said, No man, you guys are too smart by half, you seem to know everything. We ought not to be afraid of saying that there are things that are mystery.
BHO: Just say I don't know?
Archbishop: And say no matter how much our knowledge gets to increase, the mystery will remain. It is not a problem that can be solved.
BHO: What do you think – as the top churchman in South Africa you've got to know the answer to this – happens when

Big Holy Chart

Top Five Ways to Achieve Immortality

The Woody Allen approach, who, when asked how he would like to achieve immortality replied, 'By not dying.' The James Dean approach ... Look cool, Live fast, Die young. The George Best approach...Look great, dribble brilliantly, play for Man United and be drunk on TV chat shows. The Jesus Christ approach....Do good, Make miracles, Die young ...and come back later in the weekend.

you die?

Archbishop: Simon, Simon, Simon ... I just don't know. I just know that there is going to be some kind of dissolution of the body and that there is a real me that remains and that gets to be something called the resurrection. I mean my life does not end with the physical dissolution of my body.

BHO: So there will be somewhere else where the real you goes?

Archbishop: What is important is that you will remain the real you. Recognisably. And not dissembodied. We believe not in the immortality of the soul but we believe in the resurrection of the body. That is to say that you Simon, will be recognisably you but you will have a body that is appropriate to this new existence.

BHO: OK, I think I understand most of that. Do you think there is a heaven and a hell ...

> Now and again you think, 'Well, it might be curtains.' But then I usually say, 'God, if I'm doing your work, you jolly well are going to have to look after me – and if you don't, tough luck!'

and who gets where?

Archbishop: Heaven is in fact to be with God and being one who seeks to reflect the nature of God and the will of God ... compassionate, gentle and caring. So it is not something that is only in the future – it is here. When these young people strive for peace and when they care about their environment and when they say they have to do something about re-distributing the resources of the world so that poor people can be cared for ... you are introducing a bit of heaven. When you bring bread to someone who is starving that is a bit of heaven there ...

BHO: But this sounds like a bit of a policitians answer, what I want to know is who

is going to get into heaven?

Archbishop: Wait, wait, wait, wait ... you said what about Hell? Hell is when we are actually struggling against ourselves and when we separate ourselves from God, from the best of which we are capable. Now I do not sit in judgement and say, 'Now you are going to hell!' Although you could say that he who chucks babies into a gas chamber cannot at that moment be a candidate for heaven – but – and this is important – our God is the kind who says, 'There is nothing unforgiveable, that you and I can never say 'Aah ... that guy, he is a first class candidate for hell.'

BHO: What about the people who shot at the demonstrators in Soweto?

Archbishop: How do you or I know that that person can't be converted, become penitent and say, 'I am sorry God'. And our God is a God who is forever looking out for the possibilities of people making a new turn. That is the glory of our faith, that it is the faith of new beginnings.

BHO: Are you scared of dying?

Archbishop: I think yes, you have a kind of apprehension. It was great fun to be around on 27th April 1994, then on May 9th 1994 when we were introducing Nelson Mandela ... but ultimately, for the Christian, death is not the final destination because of the glorious resurrection of Jesus Christ. I know, I believe that I have a life that has already begun which is not going to end with death, that death is the door to a fuller life.

BHO: Have you ever come close to dying when you were on demonstrations? When you preached at these big funerals you've been a lot closer to death than most people, does that influence you?

Archbishop: Now and again you think, 'Well, it might be curtains.' But then I usually say, 'God, if I'm doing your work, you jolly well are going to have to look after me – and if you don't, tough luck!'

Dean Inge, a famous churchman, once received an anonymous letter from a lady, who wrote: 'I am praying for your death. I have been very successful in two other instances.'

Dead Elvis

According to a recent study, when Elvis Presley was alive there were 34 Elvis impersonators. Now there are 8,029. The report calculated that at the current rate, one out of every five people on earth will be an Elvis impersonator by the year 2037.

Eternity is a terrible thought. I mean, where's it going to end?
Tom Stoppard.

Drive-Thru Death

A Chicago funeral home has set up a drive-through service complete with cameras and sound system which allows visitors to pay their last respects, sign the funeral register and view the remains of a friend or loved one – all without leaving their own car.
A complex system of switches and relays allows as many as a dozen bodies to be viewed. Owner Lafayette Gatling originally came up with the idea because he used to feel uncomfortable coming to a funeral home in soiled clothes. But he says the system has been particularly helpful when the deceased was having an affair and both a wife and a girlfriend wanted to pay respects.

WHEN GROUCHO MARX WAS ASKED WHAT IT FELT LIKE TO BE NINETY YEARS OLD HE REPLIED THAT IT WAS BETTER THAN THE ALTERNATIVE.

'This way, the girlfriend can go through the drive-through and pay her respects in whatever name she chooses, while the wife is inside with the deceased. It happens all the time.'

Parishioners are requested to cut the grass around their own graves.
Parish magazine

Dead Funny: Woody Allen

I don't mind dying, I just don't want to be there when it happens.
The difference between sex and death is that with death you can do it alone and no one is going to make fun of you.
When asked how he would like to achieve immortality, he replied, 'By not dying'.
Dying is one of the few things that can be done just as easily lying down.

Dead and Buried ...in the Car

According to the Fortean Times Magazine, the ashes of beer distributor George Swanson were placed in the drivers seat of his beloved 1984 Chevrolet Corvette, which was buried as 50 mourners looked on. There were two driving caps on the back seat, red roses on the roof and Engelbert Humperdinks 'Release Me' ready to play in the cassette recorder. The car had done only 27,000 miles. 'You have a lot of people saying they want to take it with them,' said George's widow Caroline. 'He took it with him.' George had bought 12 burial plots to make sure there was room when his time came.

Dead Dawg

Margaret Roythorne looked on in horror as her tiny Cairn terrier Fynn was sucked up and killed by a mobile 'poop-scooper' in her local park in Hastings. The 7-year-old dog was run over by the vacuum muck-collector after dashing out from under some bushes.

BEREAVEMENT

JANE: I don't know what I'm going to do about this stain, Marge.

MARGE: Let's have a look. Mmm, nasty. What is it?

JANE: Bereavement. Lost my husband two years ago. I'm still devastated.

MARGE: Not for long you aren't!

JANE: But it's one of those deep-down traumas, Marge. It'll never shift. Marge, I'm clinically depressed.

MARGE: And this, Jane, is clinically proven Pretend. Watch. (ZING!)

JANE: Ooh, Marge, it's just wonderful, with this Pretend the gut wrenching psychic and emotional pain has completely gone. ... I feel so ... happy. So ... very very happy. I'm not missing Colin at all ... really ...

ANNOUNCER: Pretend. Why not? Available wherever you look.

Death and The After-Life – An Insiders Guide

1 Almost every society has some belief in survival after death – with the minor exception of some modern Western countries like Britain and America.

The basic possibilities include

- a continuation of life with little change in the nature of existence,

- a series of lives and deaths before ultimate extinction,

- moral improvement through a series of stages or 'planes'

- bodily resurrection at some future date.

2 Alongside belief in a future life you often get belief in Reincarnation – the idea that Sylvester Stallone will come back as an actor or John Major will come back as a convincing Prime Minister.

Adherents to Krishna Consciousness ('Harry Rama, Harry Enfield' etc) believe that after death the soul is reincarnated. The way one lives this life will determine the form one will have in the next life.

Another bunch into reincarnation are followers of Meher Baba, the self-proclaimed Messiah from India who never said a word for 43 years and counted Pete Townshend of The Who amongst his devotees. Mr Baba, who claimed to be the final and greatest incarnation of God – this was despite contradictory claims being made at the time about Eric Clapton – said that man's soul begins as a stone and then moves into metal, and eventually – via vegetables, insects, reptiles, fish, birds and animals – the soul moves from a monkey to a human being.

Mr Baba, no relation to Babar the Elephant, said that there are seven planes of human existence and if a person misues his spiritual powers as he works his way up to the fifth plane of sainthood, he could be sent all the way back to a stone in his next incarnation. The sixth plane is the plane of illumination and the final one is Nirvana, merger into the mind of God. Nevermind.

3 Many tribal societies have beliefs about the after-life – but often pretty vague ones, they're not bothered about exactly how many jewels they get in their crown. Some of them think that there it is pretty much as it is here – which seems a bit unambitious really.

They don't always locate The Land of the Dead in the heavens – it's often under the earth, like the Zulu's who believe in an underworld, with mountains and rivers and dead people living in villages and milking their cattle – the cattle incidentally are the spirits of the cattle which have been killed on earth. A kind of spirit-milk, whiskey perhaps. Mmmm, nice.

4 In Hinduism marriage is linked to death because it ensures not only the continuity of the family but also the welfare of the family's dead members in the other world. Only a son can perform the funeral rites which provide the soul of his dead father with a new spiritual body with which to pass on to the next life.

Families are important to the followers of Sun Myung Moon too – The Moonies believe that the faithful will enter the kingdom of heaven in families. Hence the importance of getting married. You singles out there, tough titty – marriage is a kind of eternal life assurance.

Incidentally, a tip for avoiding the Hindu hell: there are three gates to Hell according to the holy book the Bhagavadgita – lust, anger and greed.

5 Religious Jews utter the Shema as their last words – Hear O Israel, the Lord our God is one God…' Some do believe in life after death and in the resurrection of the body but Judaism is mainly concerned with this life, not the next one.

6 Although not that many people go to church these days, Christian ideas about the afterlife remain strong for many people in Britain. 'He's in a better place now,' – that kind of thing. Christian beliefs include judgement after death – just outside the Pearly Gates – and a subsequent assignment for a rather indeterminate period, to either Heaven or Hell.

Whether you make it to Heaven depends on whether you faithfully followed Jesus while on earth or how good a person you were… slight theological differences here.

Many Christians believe in a discarnate state after death that is followed by a resurrection in the body at the time of the second coming of Christ. Christians claim that just as Jesus overcame death by being resurrected after the crucifixion – so can his followers.

Crucifixes are sexy because there's a naked man on them. Madonna

12 APOSTLES THIMBLES. Set of 12 thimbles beautifully picture Jesus' 12 disciples. Exquisitely detailed porcelain thimbles display the name and likeness of each Apostle. Makes a unique display to be cherished forever.

B9721 Apostles Thimbles   Set of 12 Was $11.98
NOW $9.85

THE WORST THING THAT I COULD THINK OF WOULD BE TO HAVE TO SPEND TWENTY FOUR HOURS AS A SCEPTIC

Mike Scott

BHO: You really were an obvious choice for a heretic of the week as soon as this new single came out where you're singing 'The great god Pan is alive.' Pan is the ancient god of life, is that right?

Heretic: Well he was a shepherd god in ancient Greece and he's known as the god of all the living creatures on earth. The god of the animals and the little creatures and there's a school of thought also that Pan is in everybody, everybody has a bit of Pan in them.

BHO: When you sing 'The great god Pan is alive', is this poetic licence or is this a literal discovery?

Heretic: Oh, it's a literal discovery, Pan is a real thing. All the ancient gods are real things and I suppose you could say they're like energies, archetypal energies and to the ancient people they appeared as gods. Now we're in a different era and we've a different way of looking at things but those things are still real.

BHO: So when you say in the song 'Guess who I've been dancing with,' was this your confrontation with Pan? What was your meeting like?

Heretic: Well I have had a number meetings with Pan and it's kinda my secret, it's not something that I like to talk about in this form, but then to put it in the songs so people can make what they can of it.

BHO: Listening to the album 'Dream Harder' you seem to have had some kind of spiritual revolution or revelation?

Heretic: Well I always believed in God ever since I was a little boy. I never had any doubt about the existence of God but I was never very good at putting my belief into practise: kind of living my beliefs. A couple of years ago I was drinking a lot and I was doing a lot of things I shouldn't and my life was kind of freewheeling down a slope and my band split up underneath me. I decided, well screw this I'm gonna get myself together, I'm gonna use whatever gifts I've been given and I'm gonna do what I think God wants me to do and in doing that I'll find out what he really wants me to do. That's what I've been doing and that's my life, that's what I'm working on.

BHO: So how did you go about finding out what God wanted you to do?

Heretic: Following my intuition first of all. I believe that everybody can find out what God wants them to do, everybody has different ways.

BHO: And which god is this? Would it be the God of your upbringing or does Pan have a say in this or is this all gods or what?

Heretic: This is just god god.

BHO: One of the songs on the album has the line 'I'm a functioning part of the masters plan,' and I was just wondering who 'the master' was? Presumably not The Master from Doctor Who?

Heretic: Nah, not that one. It's not any particular master it's just God. God is thousands of names, every culture on earth calls god by a different name. Now I'm not a subscriber to any specific religion, like my friend Karl Wallinger I'm completely non-denominational. I just

ALL THE ANCIENT GODS ARE REAL THINGS AND I SUPPOSE YOU COULD SAY THEY'RE LIKE ENERGIES, ARCHETYPAL ENERGIES AND TO THE ANCIENT PEOPLE THEY APPEARED AS GOD

believe in God, I believe there's one power that created the world and the universe and there are many ways to know that power, you can know God through love or through the heart or through nature but it's all one God.

BHO: Is this like Mike Scottism, have you developed your own religion?

Heretic: No not at all, I'm too much of an idiot for that.

BHO: Your song 'Spiritual City', is this New York where you've been living of late?

Heretic: Well I wrote it before I moved to New York, but it's turned out that New York is my kind of spiritual city. I've learned a lot in my own spiritual journey since I've been here, I've learned to meditate. Everyday I'm learning something new and becoming more aware of the things that come between me and God, my own hang-ups and insecurities and I'm working through them and I've been doing most of that in New York. Sure there's rapists and muggers and pan-handlers in the city but there's also great life and light and love as well. On balance you get the worst and best in the same place.

BHO: Do you visit a temple or synagogue or church to take your spiritual journey further?

Heretic: I kind of get into it in my own backyard. I learned to meditate last year and that's been a great thing for me, so I do that every morning and every night in my own house. It's a search for inner peace which in itself is also a journey towards something.

BHO: And how far are you along that journey?

Heretic: Pathetic, but I'm working on it. But I'm much happier and more solid, It's like I'm standing on a rock. That's an old biblical connotation but I don't mean it that way. I'm standing on a rock. Like everyone else I've got my own insecurities and problems but I feel confident that I can work them out and I've got this resource inside of me, especially through meditation, that I can turn to if things get tough for me.

BHO: Finally we do have to ask you for a form of torture, because there is is a fine English tradition of burning people who we disagree with, who stray from the norm and you certainly stray from most norms.

Heretic: The worst thing that I could think of would be to have to spend twenty four hours as a sceptic.

GODBOX

In America they have launched a special accessory for the Christian Television Set. Its transparent, you hang it on the top of your screen and, a Bible verse stares you in the eye as you are looking at the box declaring, 'I Will Set No Wicked Thing Before My Eyes' – that's from Psalm 103 incidentally. The manufacturers says that 'with so much on television that is of the flesh, that wars against the spirit', this is a powerful yet quiet reminder from the Bible to keep the viewing clean.

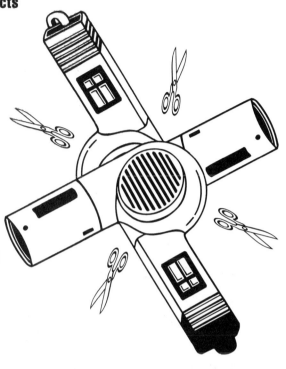

The Big Holy Guide to

Krishna Consciousness

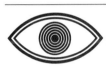

Hare Krishna is the nickname for Gaudiya Vaisnavism, a Hindu religion, the followers of which don't gamble or consume alcohol, coke, fish, eggs or have sex before marriage.

There are 5,000 of them in Britain, most of them wandering up and down London's Oxford Street in red nighties chanting Hare Krishna.

Hare Krishna's believe the body is temporary, that people may be reincarnated as animals and that the soul is for cultivating a relationship with God – Lord Krishna. Much to the dismay of the locals, up to fifteen hundred people a week visit Bachtivendanta, the sects British HQ, a 30-room Georgian Manor in Hertfordshire bought by Beatle George Harrison who also wrote the Krishna consciousness hit, My Sweet Lord. Hare Krishna's attract a lot of George's – Boy George recently converted.

Hare Krishnas worship the Tulsi plant from the Sweet Basil family. In the early nineties Kalindi, a sacred Hare Krishna cow who lived at Bachtivendanta, died after miraculously producing 12,000 litres of milk for trainee priests there – without ever having a calf.

Big Holy Chart

Top Five Religious Haircuts

In at number five this week the Hare Krishna totally shaved with tiny pig-tail cut.

At number four, for the second week running, the pudding-basin and humorously placed central bald patch monastic look.

Down at three the out-of-date yuppie pony-tail now appearing on the heads of trendy Anglican vicars.

At number two, its the ever-popular rastafarian dreadlocks – stitch-on or home-grown.

But still at Number One in this week's top five religious haircuts nothing goes quite so well with a black coat and hat as the lovingly curled ringlets of the Hasidic Jewish community.

MUM & TERENCE

TERENCE: Here, Mum –

MUM: Yes, Terence?

TERENCE: Why does Daddy always say a prayer before he preaches a sermon?

MUM: He's asking God to help him, dear.

TERENCE: Oh, I see. Yeah. So … er … Mum…?

MUM: … Yes dear?

TERENCE: Why doesn't God help him?

MUM: Terence, dear –

TERENCE: Yes, Mum?

MUM: Do other children laugh at you because your Dad's a vicar?

TERENCE: No Mum, no – not at all. They like him.

MUM: Do they know he's a vicar?

TERENCE: Not exactly, Mum, no.

MUM: I hope you don't lie.

TERENCE: Oh no Mum, I don't lie. I tell 'em he cross-dresses at weekends. They reckon that's really cool.

TERENCE: Here, Mum –

MUM: Yes, dear?

TERENCE: I've found out what a preacher is.

MUM: A great blessing to us all, Terence.

TERENCE: No. Someone who talks in other people's sleep …

TERENCE: Here, Mum?

MUM: Yes dear?

TERENCE: What was all that in church this morning about money?

MUM: It's called a 'thermometer appeal', darling.

TERENCE: A thermometer appeal?

MUM: Yes dear – we're raising funds to buy a big thermometer all of our very own … like other churches have …

TERENCE: Here, Mum?

MUM: Yes, dear?

TERENCE: Hear of someone called Gandhi?

MUM: I think he was an Indian gentleman, dear.

TERENCE: Someone asked him, you see, what he thought of Western Civilisation – and he said, 'I think it would be a very good idea.'

MUM: Yes – well he probably didn't understand the question, dear …

I met this guy once in a mental hospital I was visiting. He introduced himself to me as Jesus Christ. I just said, 'Haven't we met before?' He said nothing. I asked him why, if he was the Son of God, was he in a mental hospital? He said, 'Because it's my 40 days and 40 nights in the wilderness.' At that point I just cracked up. I asked him when the end of the world was going to come. He said April 1st. I thought, 'Brilliant, pencil it into the diary. The world will end on April Fool's Day. Perfect.'

Bono, singer

The Rev. Jim Mahin will preach on the religious aspects of the movie "Mary Poppins" and members of the congregation will present scenes from the musical at 9 a.m. and 10:30 a.m. Sunday at Palisades United Methodist Church, 27002 Camino De Estrella, Capistrano Beach.

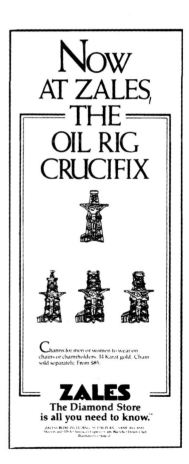

DOES WHAT THE CHURCH SAYS ON MORAL ISSUE INFLUENCE YOU IN ANY WAY AT ALL IN YOUR OWN DECISION MAKING?

HOW MANY OF THE TEN COMMANDMENTS CAN YOU REMEMBER?

IF KEEPING THE SABBATH AND BLASPHEMING SEEM A BIT OLD HAT, WHAT DO YOU THINK SHOULD BE INCLUDED IN A TEN COMMANDMENTS FOR THE 1990'S ?

WHAT IS COVETOUSNESS ANYWAY?

WOULD YOU RATHER JOHN MAJOR OR OPRAH WINFREY CAME UP WITH A NEW SET OF COMMANDMENTS FOR THE NINETIES?

DO THE RIGHT THING?

Crisis, what crisis? Everyone says there's a moral crisis in Britain so The Big Holy One asked MORI, the poll people, to find out if young people think there is a crisis. You had to be out of the country to avoid hearing the results – they were plastered everywhere.

Here's what we found.

Two-thirds of young people said that their generation is experiencing a moral crisis and that 'they are not sure what is right and wrong.'

Only a tiny percentage of them said that Government ministers or politicians are doing a good job of setting and upholding moral standards. More than two thirds said that they are not influenced by what the Church says on right and wrong.

The poll discovered that people between the ages of 15 and 35 could recall less than three of the Ten

Commandments and, when shown them all, only considered an average of five were important any longer. Not murdering, not stealing, and respecting your parents remain important but religious commandments like worshipping God were viewed as largely irrelevant.

The results of the poll were published smack in the middle of the Party Political Conference Season, but Conservative MP's could not play their usual card and take refuge in saying that the Church has to give firmer moral leadership in society.

More than half of those polled said that 'the Church has little to offer people nowadays' and only one in seven said the Church has any influence on what they think is right and wrong.

Barely half of those polled said that 'there are definite rights and wrongs in life' – more than 40% said it 'depends on the circumstances'.

More than half said that Parliament and politicians are doing a bad job at 'setting and upholding moral standards' – only 4% said they

THE **NEW** TEN COMMANDMENTS

(well … by popular approval …)

DON'T KILL	87%
DON'T DRINK AND DRIVE	79%
DON'T STEAL	73%
TREAT OTHERS AS YOU'D LIKE TO BE TREATED YOURSELF	71%
DON'T BE VIOLENT	70%
DON'T BE RACIST	68%
CARE FOR THE ENVIRONMENT	64%
DON'T TAKE DRUGS	60%
BE LOYAL TO YOUR FRIENDS	55%
ONLY HAVE SEX WITH YOUR HUSBAND OR WIFE	53%

AND A FEW MORE WHICH AREN'T SO POPULAR

Don't be sexist	51%	Tony Blair	6%
Don't own a gun	44%	Margaret thatcher	6%
Always tell the truth	39%	Paddy Ashdown	5%
Don't sleep around	38%	Anita Roddick	4%
Don't fiddle taxes	25%	Sting	4%
Don't have gay sex	20%	The Chief Rabbi	3%
Don't smoke	19%	John Major	2%
Don't use porn	17%	The Levellers	2%
Love God	16%	Madonna	1%
Don't swear	15%		
Don't have sex before marriage	7%		
Go to church regularly	7%		

Who would you trust to come up with a new set of commandments for the nineties?

MotherTheresa	25%
The Pope	17%
The Archbishop of Canterbury	13%
Richard Branson	12%
Oprah WInfrey	12%
David Bellamy	11%
Prince Charles	9%
Bob Geldof	9%

Who sets a good moral example?

Schools	34%
Doctors	27%
Parents	32%
Police	32%
Church	19%

Who sets a bad moral example?

Parliament and Politicians	52%
Government ministers	48%
National newspapers	46%
Royal Family	41%
Television	40%

Two in three said that the younger generation is experiencing a moral crisis

did a good job. Nearly half said that Government ministers in particular were doing a bad job – only 3% said they did a good job.

Doctors, parents and the police were widely viewed as doing a good job at maintaining moral standards, only 6% said that the Royal Family or national newspapers were doing a good job.

If the Church was once an institution expected to rinforce the moral fibre of the nation, it now fares poorly in the perceptions of 15-35 year olds. A majority said that the 'Church has little to offer people nowadays' with less than a quarter disagreeing with this.

Only one in seven said that 'what the church says about what is morally right and wrong' has a strong influence on my life'.

But at least religious figures came up well when people were asked who they would trust to come up with a new set of commandments for the nineties – The Pope, Mother Teresa and the Archbishop of Canterbury led the way with John Major getting only 2%.

Two in three said that the younger generation is experiencing a moral crisis. One in five disagreed.

Just over half (52%) said there are invariable rights and wrongs but two in five (41%) said there were not.

The majority of people (61%) said that people should be allowed to do whatever they like so long as it doesn't harm anyone. Less than a third disagreed.

Young people who believe in God – of some kind or another – are more likely to think there are definite rights and wrongs (58%) and less likely to think that people should be allowed to do whatever they like (55%). More of them also thought that there was a moral crisis in the younger generation (70%) than those who did not.

Most people can recall fewer than three of the Ten Commandments. They tend to remember the ones they think are important (Don't murder, don't steal). The commandments about respecting God are generally regarded as the least important, with Keeping the Sabbath in last place with less than one in ten thinking it was still important.

The majority of 15-35 year olds say they are Christian both in upbringing and current practice. But only two thirds (67%) of those with a broadly Christian background still practice or believe Christianity.

Just over half believe in a God of some form (52%), while one in seven do not think there is a God (15%). The remainder are uncommitted but belief in a God is more widespread among young women (60%) than men (43%).

RATS

Tory: The spiritual legacy of the 1980's is surely that there is no such thing as society. Each of us must stand alone. After all, rats in a cage don't waste time looking around and asking if everybody is all right. They fight tooth and claw to win – because if they don't win, they die – a simple truth, and surely one which lies at the very heart of

Big Things Come in Little Packages!

Jesus' story of the Good Samaritan …

Announcer: Believing Jesus' voted Conservative. One of life's little comforts.

R: So God, no offence or anything but not that many people believing in you these days, or feeling any sort of relationship or attachment to you. How do you feel?

G: It makes me very cross.

R – Oh. A sort of angry diety breathing fury and destruction eh? 'God In Thunderbolt Shock Threat.'

G: No, you misunderstand. It makes me very cross. It crucifies me.

R: (embarrassed) Oh, so not just another day in paradise for you then?

G: Your words …

Derek: Nah. They shouldn't print that. Call me old-fashioned and that but really …

Dave: Let's have a look then. Oh, yeah. No, that's tacky …

Derek: And degrading. We don't want to see women doing that.

Dave: She's on page seventeen as well, it says here. So we could turn to it and see if she's doing more things that we don't want to see …

Derek: Alright, alright, careful, it's my magazine …

Dave: Yeah, but I saw what page it was on.

Derek: No. They should definitely not print that. That I do not want to see.

Dave: Well, don't hog it Derek, remember I don't want to see it either …

Big Holy Chart

Top Five Modern Translations of the Ten Commandments

- Thou Shall Not Bear False Witness becomes, in modern parlance 'being economical with the truth'
- Thou shallt not commit adultery becomes 'I'm working late at the office tonight darling … don't wait up.'
- Keep The Sabbath Holy becomes 'Well, if you can't go to Safeways on a Sunday, what kind of a society are we living in …'
- Respect your mother and father … as long as they don't embarass you in front of your friends in which case you may need to give them a severe and public shouting at …
- Thou Shalt not Take the Name of the Lord in Vain … becomes 'Oh Christ Almighty, Oh God, you won't believe it for Christ's Sake … I've forgotten to set the video recorder to tape Baywatch.'

Top Five Signs Your Heading for a Marital Difficulties

- You have a black eye and broken nose and you can't remember what a condom looks like
- You've started writing to Marjorie Proops
- Your partner's been sleeping at her parents for three months … even though she was raised in a childrens home.
- She says she hopes that is a pistol in your pocket because you needn't bother bringing it out if its anything else …
- The marriage guidance counsellors said that they were sorry but in this instance they really couldn't help …

PERSONAL RESPONSIBILITY

D: There's a lot of evasion going Dave.

Dave: How do you mean Derek?

Derek: Moral decline in Britain – and I just feel a lot of people are evading personal responsibility.

Dave: Right. Sort of saying, 'It's nothing to do with me! ' That sort of thing.

Derek: That sort of thing, yeah. But I, Derek, take my responsibilty seriously.

Dave: You, Derek, do.

Derek: In the end, in any moral crisis, we have to inspect ourselves and come to a personal decision.

Dave: Right, and now you have, er, inspected yourself, what is your personal decision …

Derek: I have personally decided to blame the

Government, the Royal Family and the Church …

Dave: You're a brave man, Derek, a brave, brave man …

HIGH GROUND

NOISY SCENE: EXCAVATORS, CROWDS, JOSTLING

J: Quick! More soil over here! Anything! Yes, those rocks will be fine. Look – get on the phone, could you? We need more excavators. We desperately need a new mound over here. And could you lot please wait! We're doing our best. You'll be allowed up soon, when we've built more. There just isn't enough room at the moment for everyone.

B: What's going on Jack?

J: Oh, it's the political party conference season and we've

run out of moral high ground

Big Holy Chart

Top Five Ways to Spot a Morally Dodgy Politician

Says he's proud to call himself a family man … but couldn't pick his own wife out at an identity parade.

Is a fervent campaigner on behalf of embattled Soho nightclubs – where he has to go to keep doing important research.

His former actress-secretarial help tells tabloid newspaper that she's sucked his toes and they all support Chelsea.

Says he smoked cannabis … but never inhaled.

Prime Minister attacks press coverage of his domestic difficulties and offers him his full support …

Politics and church are the same thing – they keep the people in ignorance.
Bob Marley, singer.

The Pop Star and The Politician
Ricky Ross and Tony Benn

Ricky Ross: This is a very excited Ricky Ross here because I'm at the home of Tony Benn, long a hero of mine, who's written some of the most inspiring socialist documents of our time and he's linked his socialism with a belief in God and the teachings of Jesus.

Tony, you're an ex-cabinet minister known to be far-left in the Labour Party, I'm a pop-singer, we're both sitting here on Radio One talking about Christianity.

A lot of people associate Christianity with the royalty, patronage, the military, the establishment in general but there is another model of Christianity which has intrigued me over recent years ... the Church in South Africa, the Church in Central America, the Church in Eastern Europe, which instead of being on the side of the establishment has actually spoken out for the poor people, the oppressed people ...

Tony Benn: I think of Jesus as the carpenter of Nazareth and the Risen Christ is a very different image. The Christian language is so obstructive. They talk about the Kingdom of God ... well I'm a Republican, I don't believe in the Kingdom of any kind. I went to do a talk to some Anglican ministers the other day and one of the evangelical ones said to me, 'Do you accept Christ as your Lord?' Well I don't believe in Lords...

Ricky: Is that a problem with language?

Tony: It's a problem with language but also the real thing isn't it? You see the Pope on his throne.

Ricky: In the Old Testament you have these amazing images of kings and prophets where they became a quite different thing that the kind we accept now ...

Tony: Well, the Old Testament kings were kings alright, the question is was Jesus a king or a prophet? I think he was a prophet. All religions begin with a flame of faith and end up with a bureaucracy. And I'm not interested in the Christian bureaucracy that burns heretics. I'm interested in the faith, same as the Labour Party, began with a flame of faith and ends up with a bureaucracy, expelling people. And that is the way that structures develop. You have to go back to the root of it all, that Jesus was a poor man who spoke for the poor ... and if you say, do you accept Jesus as my Shop Steward or Jesus as my teacher then yes, but not Jesus as my lord or king. That language is obstructive to understanding, but more than that it reflects the way Christian leaders see themselves. Now in liberation theology in Latin America, the first commandment is 'feed the poor' and the Scottish churches have always been involved in the ecumenical movement and I think that's the way we should look at religion, not in terms of splendid people in mitres and copes and all the rest of it.

Ricky: But who are people going to learn that from, do they go back to the Bible or what?

Tony Benn: The Church of England is our oldest nationalised industry, Henry VIII nationalised it because he had a row with the Pope and he wanted a priest in every pulpit every Sunday telling you that God

> I WENT TO DO A TALK TO SOME ANGLICAN MINISTERS THE OTHER DAY AND ONE OF THE EVANGELICAL ONES SAID TO ME, 'DO YOU ACCEPT CHRIST AS YOUR LORD?' WELL I DON'T BELIEVE IN LORDS.

PEOPLE TALK ABOUT THE KINGDOM OF GOD...

WELL I'M A REPUBLICAN, I DON'T BELIEVE IN THE KINGDOM OF ANY KIND.

wanted you to do what the king wanted you to do ... you can see why he did it. So you have to understand that the control of thought is an integral part of government and the use of religion to control thought and secure obedience is what it was all about. Cutting the links of church and state, which is an integral part of the American Constitution, liberates the church to be what it ought to be and then you do get a church of the people and not a church of the mighty. If that were to happen, you'd find the Christian message spread quite rapidly.

She was an atheist and I was an agnostic. We didn't know what religion not to bring our children up in. **Woody Allen**

Big Holy Chart

Top Five Designer Religions

At number five, on the way down, its Buddhism offering salvation for Suzanne Vega, Boy George, Lynne Franks, Sandie Shaw and Tina Turner.

At four it's a new entry for Islam with Muhammed Ali, Cat Stevens, Richard Thompson and, thought to be on the brink, boxer Mike Tyson. Straight in at three its Free Presbyterianism the Wee Free's – which works its legalistic magic for the Lord Chancellor himself, Lord Mackay of Clashfern.

At two it's Roman Catholicism, rumoured to be the preferred choice of the Holy Father himself, Pope John Paul II.

But way out in front at number one it's U2 and The Church of Frisbeeterians. As Bono explained, 'We believe that when you die your soul goes up on the roof and you can't get it down again.'

Top Five Celebrity Religious Celibates

At number five this week its Wimbledon champion Andre Agassi of whom Smash Hits magazine reported 'sex is out of the question, he's a devout Christian'.

At number four this week its Mother Teresa of Calcutta because living saints don't have time for fleshly pursuits.

Down at number three its those 34 Buddhist monks just returned from four years secluded meditation removed from any traces of the opposite sex. At number two its the Pope. He may be called the Holy Father but he never will be because celibacy is part of the job-description.

And at number one for the for the second millenium running its Cliff Richard because, well, he's Cliff Richard.

Top Five Most Unwanted Religious Posts

Down to number five this week it's any female member of the Children of God cult who have to go 'hooking for Jesus' not knowing what dirty old fish they end up catching.

In at number four in the most unwanted religious posts it's the ever-unpopular PR person for Tammy Faye Bakker.

Tied at number three, its a missionary posting to the Antarctic or Chaplain to the Atheist Society of Great Britain.

Up at number two its any lead guitarist in a Christian heavy metal band

And at number one for the 200th week running its Special Envoy of the Archbishop of Canterbury – which can lead to several years solitary confinement in Beirut.

LURVE

LONE VOICE OF WHISPERED PASSION

A: I love you. You know that, don't you? But I'm going to tell you again ... I love you. I love you so much ... and you love me too. I know you do. I see it. I feel it. And now I want to please you. Pleasure you. I'll do anything. I want to give you pleasure ... for ... for ... forever.

Announcer: The Church of England. Where people make lurve ... every week...

Christians have been portrayed as fearful, judgemental, condemning people trying to play God

Maria McKee

BHO: Maria, you're a big holy sister now and the reason we've dragged you in is you've got a new album out called 'You've Gotta Sin To Get Saved' ... the idea behind the title is what?

Heretic: Well I guess its pretty much what it says; it's a play on words. I was brought up in a gospel environment and tunes and phrases like that are sort of easy on my ear personally. I guess what it means is that sometimes you have to be wrong to be right you know. For me singing is very much a religious experience just in general.

BHO: How d'you mean?

Heretic: I look at my voice as a kind of gift in a way from God and so when I sing it feels like some kind of communication.

BHO: In some press articles I've seen, you are called a 'born-again-rocker.'

Heretic: Yeah if you wanna call it born again, I'd say that's what I believe in. I read the Bible every day and stuff like that. So

yeah I'm Christian. It's tough to go out and talk about it because Christians have been portrayed in the media as these fearful, judgemental, condemning, people trying to play god and expecting perfection from the human race ... and they don't even take the time to look at their own lives and to be one on one with God. It's always me and the rest of the world ... t has nothing to do with the true message of Christianity which I think is love, compassion and tolerance, brotherhood and unity and all that stuff. But that's just been swept aside and corrupted by greed and power and anger and fear. So I'm actually reluctant at times to say I'm a Christian.

BHO: Because of the connotations?

Heretic: Yeah the term 'born-again-Christian' – people automatically say 'Oh you're a republican' or 'Oh, you voted for George Bush ... because the lines have been blurred for so long.

Liam of Hothouse Flowers

BHO: Liam the dedication on your album reads 'To God and the land from which all that keeps us alive comes many thanks, thank you.' Why did you put that on?

Liam: Well god, for whatever it means to anybody is the creative force that is around us; and the land, I wanted to remind people that what we're standing on is what keeps us alive, no matter how much money there is around. If the land runs out then the money's pretty useless.

BHO: Any particular god, any particular land?

Liam: No. The land; and god. God might have a hundred thousand names, might be atheism to the atheist as somebody once said.

BHO: Van Morrison, U2, Clannad, Deacon Blue, The Proclaimers – there seems to be greater spirituality to a lot of Celtic music. Would you go along with that? Is it just just a vibe or a culture or something more specific and personal?

Liam: Well Ireland is a country that has been known for spiritual thought for centuries. One thing is that we haven't been writing for that long; most of our knowledge has been oral up until only two hundred years ago we used to just carry our information from person to person from father to son from generation to generation. I think that's where a lot of improvisation, poetic improvisation comes from. I learned most of my music orally. Songs I was taught by ear and music I was also taught by ear.

My own spirituality really comes from what's around me. I'm a swimmer, I swim in the morning in the sea, most mornings if I can. That's one of my primary rituals, just peace of mind and contact with water and contact with the nature that I believe I am part of.

BHO: So it's like a theology of swimming really?

Liam: It's a great addiction because it's not bad for you.

BHO: I was reading in this months 'Q' about your trip to South Africa where you were playing to tiny village in Zululand. It was quite clearly a roots music concert because you had your didgeridoo and the reporter who was with you was saying that the crowd really got off on the traditional stuff you were doing as opposed to tracks from the new album. Do you think there's a spirituality there that you pick up in different countries of the world?

Liam: Yeah, music is a reflection of people and the more basic the music is, the more it reflects those people. I found having come from a country that has not been allowed to practise her language or her faith or her ways for about five hundred years or has been persecuted for that, we Irish have an understanding of people such as the Native Americans and people such as the Africans and the understanding isn't really in words it's in music.

My spirituality is music. I suppose at the end of the day music is one of the greatest teachers, one of the greatest binders in a lot of ways I've a lot to be grateful for that I can do it.

My spirituality is music – one of the greatest teachers.

John Peel

The Last Judgement

BHO: Have you ever had a religious experience?

Peel: Well there are two ways of approaching all of this, the facetious side of me would say seeing Alan Kennedy's shot go into the back of the net in the Parc de Prince when Liverpool were in the European Cup against Real Madrid would be as close as I'd ever come. But on a serious level No! Although somebody once tipped me as the kind of rather obsessive bloke who was likely to have one and I live in fear of it to be honest with you Simon because it's the uncertainty of life that I find attractive.

BHO: Do you ever pray?

Peel: Not really no.

BHO: Who's the most holy person you've ever met?

Peel: Well again I was very tempted to say Bill Shankley 'cause I once carried his bags from a hotel to a tour bus but in fact I would say, and this will embarrass him considerably, my father-in-law. He's just one of those people who's first thought is of other people, and there are a decreasing number of people like that alas.

BHO: What music would you like played at your funeral?

Peel: I should like things like the Undertones Teenage Kicks but then Sheila my wife said that that would remind her so much of me that it would make her even more sad than if we played something like some rather grim cello concerto or something. I don't really know. Something rousing though.

BHO: Have you ever bought the War Cry or the Watchtower?

Peel: I have actually, because although as I say I'm a heathen fundamentalist, I do have a lot of admiration for the Salvation Army as an institution and when I was a very nervous and confused and unhappy 17-year-old boy soldier in a camp on Salisbury Plain, the people who ran the Salvation Army canteen there took me in in a way and were really good to me so I buy their magazines both for that reason and also because they have rather a good easy sort of quick crossword too.

BHO: Who would you like to spend eternity with?

Peel: Just members of my family. My mum died last year and I was very sad about that obviously. The only reason that I would care for there to be an after life is so that I can talk to her about some of the things that I forgot to say to her when she was still alive really.

BHO: And our final question to the national broadcaster of the year John Peel. What is heaven like and are you going there?

Peel: I can't really envisage the traditional view of heaven where you sit around and sing songs to the Lord. It seems to me a rather dull way of spending your time, so heaven to me is sort of sitting out in the garden on a sunny evening with a bottle of wine surrounded by indifferent members of the family, with the prospect of an Indian take-away in the not-too-distant future.

Heaven to me is sort of sitting out in the garden on a sunny evening with a bottle of wine

Ritual Abuse

Derek: I mean, this ritual abuse business ... it's beyond the pale, basically, the things they do ...

Dave: Oh right ...

Derek: Hardly believe it possible ...

Dave: So what do they do exactly?

Derek: What? In ritual abuse?

Dave: Yeah. I mean, you hear a lot about it and all that but what do they actually do?

Derek: Oh well, obviously I can only divulge that which I can divulge ...

Dave: Obviously ...

Derek: But I mean what I can say is that there is a lot of ritual involved...

Dave: Oh right.

Derek: And that obviously it is a very abusive ritual

Dave: What – you mean they sort of chant the abuse?

Derek: That's the sort of thing yeah. There tends to be some sort of musical setting to the nasty words, yeah...

Dave: And what's that er ... sat ... santanic ... er ...?

Derek: You mean Santana ritual abuse, I think.

Dave: Oh, that's it yeah.

Derek: Well, obviously Santana ritual abuse is a very particular sort involving overlong guitar solos from boring old farts who had their last hit in 1971.

Dave: Oh, that must be terrible.

Derek: Beyond the pale in my book, frankly Dave ...

Strange But True

Dead Weird

A Buddhist monk in Thailand has been stripped of his saffron robes after police arrested him making love to the body of a woman during her three day funeral rites. Police were only able to charge the monk with damaging the coffin as they could not find a law barring sex with a corpse.

When I was tiny my grandmother used to beg me not to go with boys, to love Jesus and be a good girl. I grew up with two images of women: the Virgin and the whore. **Madonna**

Jesus Dollar

In the US you can now get an utterly real and authentic dollar bill with the face of Jesus stamped on it. According to the makers, when you receive your genuine Jesus dollar bill, it will be the luckiest day of your life. Their advert announces, 'On all US money are the mighty words, In God We Trust. This is to remind you to always put your Trust and Faith in the Power of God to Bless you with good Fortune, Love, Money and Happiness for the Holy Bible tells you Money Answereth All Things. Now when you have your very own Lucky Jesus Dollar, you will become a winner in life and you will never, ever be broke again.'
Only one snag. The Jesus dollar is only available by Mail Order and each one costs $5.

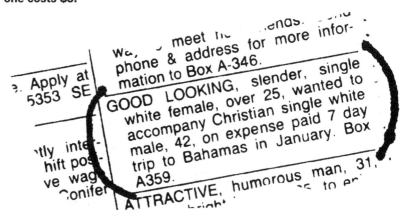

LOVELY FUNERAL

Beryl: No, I thought that was a really lovely funeral … I really did.

Brenda: It was yeah, nice vicar, wasn't he?

Beryl: Oh ever so nice, you know, the things he said … like the way he said that Albert lived a life…

Brenda: Yeah, that was ever so penetrating – although he did call him MIke at that point -

Beryl: He did yeah, but he was trying wasn't he … and then after saying that he lived a life … then he said that Albert had died now … which I thought was very good …

Brenda: Yeah, that was good, yeah, although it was just after that that he called him John, I think …

Beryl: I think you're right, yeah, but to me, do you know what?

Brenda: What?

Beryl: It was almost like he actually knew him…actually knew Albert.

Brenda: It was like that – it was just like that.

Beryl: Cos although he referred to him as Sheila in the blessing -

Brenda: We knew what he meant, didn't we?

Beryl: Yeah, we did, yeah…

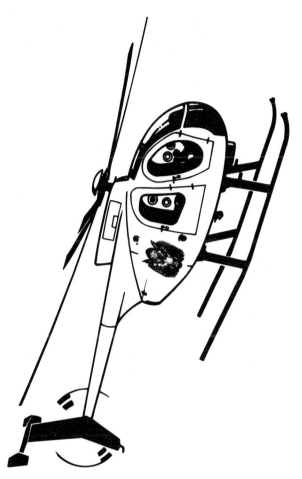

I think we're all capable of becoming the worst – the child molester, the murderer, the thief. Not to admit it is to go mad. We must steer a middle course and say, 'Yes, I have this potential but I also have the opposite potential – to be St Francis of Assisi.' We have Genghis Khan on one side and St Francis on the other and to steer a course between the two is sanity. Sting, rock singer

I loved nuns when I was growing up. I thought they were beautiful. For several years I wanted to be a nun. I saw them as really pure, disciplined, above average people. They had these serene faces. Nuns are sexy.
Madonna

THIS IS THE MAN…

ANNOUNCER:This is the man who bet Gamblers Anonymous that they couldn't cure his brother …

This is the man who said, '… and pigs will fly …' to a burly and rather aggressive police helicopter pilot …

This is the man who bought a cheap parachute because the ad said 'no strings attached …'

This is the man who had one too many at Barry's leaving do and was carried home in only his socks … by the mayor's wife …

… And this is the man who on Sunday goes to church and discovers he's not a complete failure after all …

MESSAGES

Scene:Medium at work with audience.

Medium: I'm sensing someone in the audience with a blue jacket … the blue jacket has very wide lapels … (gasps from audience, getting louder and louder). It's made of nylon … and beneath it is a bright orange shirt … and a purple tie. I'm seeing a purple tie … and flared trousers, yes, I see flared trousers now … and I smell Brut … much Brut … and difficult hair, greasy hair, very greasy … and a name, I'm getting a name … and the name is Malcolm (audience gasps reaching climax) Malcolm, I have a message for you from your wife …

Malcolm: A message from my wife?! What is it!?

Medium: She says she's really glad she's dead …

Perhaps some of the adverts in this book have lifted your spirit.

If you would like more information about The Door please write to PO Box 616, Mount Morris, Il, 61054-7610, USA